W9-BYQ-288

artful ways with
mixed
media

monique day–wilde & angie franke

STACKPOLE
BOOKS

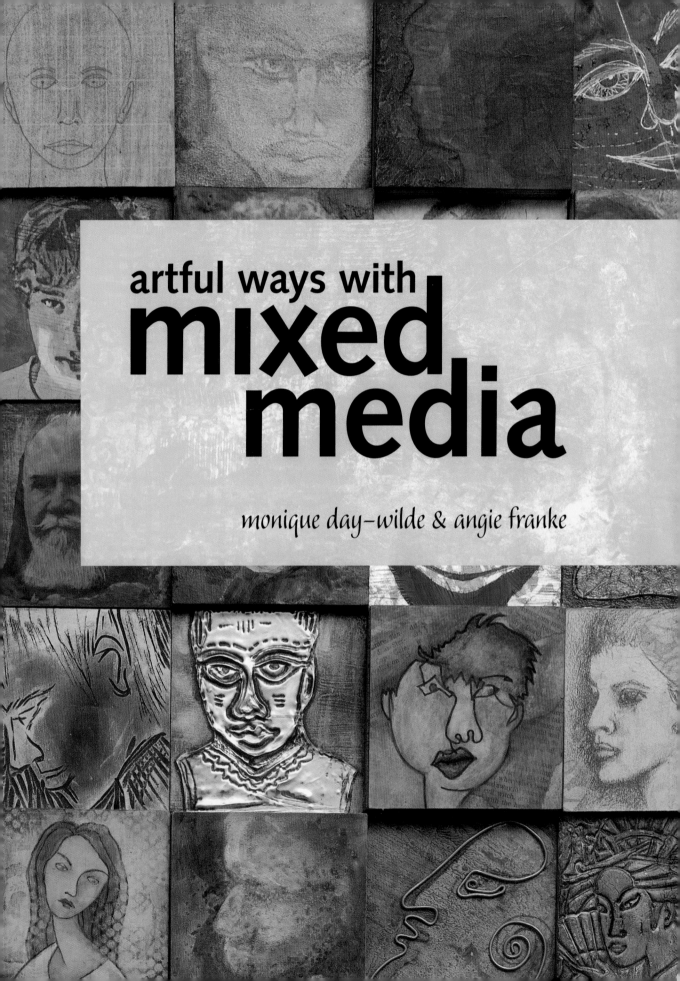

artful ways with
mixed
media

monique day–wilde & angie franke

Published by Stackpole Books
5067 Ritter Road
Mechanicsburg, PA 17055
www.stackpolebooks.com

First published in 2011
by Metz Press
1 Cameronians Avenue
Welgemoed, 7530
South Africa

Publisher   Wilsia Metz
Design and lay-out Liezl Maree
Photographer   Ivan Naudé
Proofreader   Amanda Taljaard
Reproduction   Robert Wong, Color/Fuzion
Print manager   Andrew de Kock
Printed and bound in Singapore by
  Tien Wah Press Ltd
ISBN 978-0-8117-1266-8

Contents

Introduction

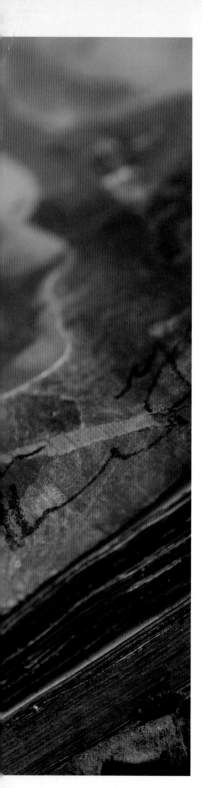

We have always worked in our own versions of mixed media, attested to by our books *Quick Art, Smart Art, Fast Art* and *Paint on Paper* amongst others. Somehow though, when talking of mixed media, the idea it conjures up is one of the layering of various media to create depth – a rich and intricate foundation on which to build an image. Paper forms an integral part of this vision together with rich colour and multi textures.

The term mixed media also brings to mind the vision of altered images and collage. When all is said and done, anything goes. We have confined our working size this time to smaller artworks and have done mostly two-dimensional examples, though the sky is the limit.

This is by no means a finite collection of possibilities, but an assortment of projects we hope will inspire you to overcome the fear of the white page. Don't be afraid to experiment: play at every opportunity and allow the creative process to grow.

We have kept this book as simple as we can, starting with a charming collage using scrapbooking media in a step by step format. Thereafter our pictures of each work's progress are presented in stages. Techniques are explained in a visual glossary referred to as 'Methods'. We chose this modus operandi so that you can mix and match your own techniques without having to refer to specific projects. We have also included a general glossary: 'Meanings'.

General hints for mixed media

- We always have the following items at hand as we use them at some time or other: masking tape, ruler, tape-measure, sandpaper, hairdryer, craft knives, cutting mat, pairs of scissors, pencils, chalk and scrap paper.
- Become a squirrel – recycle. Putting this type of artwork together requires a little collection: gather interesting images from your own picture taking, magazines, flyers, etc. Do make some sort of filing system, though, so you can find them when you need them.
- Start some sort of visual diary, journal or even scraps of paper (we're good at this) to make a collection of your images, writing and whatever else you can think of – post haste.
- Be aware of copyright as you collect items. You may have to rework stuff in artful ways to get around this very important point.

Ways with mixed media

In mixed media it's almost expected to incorporate collected items. This can pose serious copyright issues as it is illegal to use images without the original artist's permission – especially if the work is for sale. However, there are many artful tricks when dealing with this such as obscuring, altering, assimilating and layering images so that they are unrecognisable from their original form.

- **Obscure:** Do this with paint, glaze, masking and decoupage. Parts of the original can be successfully hidden with layers of melted wax, glued paper (cut, torn or tissue), card, board and found items, etc.
- **Alter:** This can be a lot of fun – draw or paint on, cut, tear, reassemble, add found items – play to your heart's content. Play, play and play some more. The more you do, the more inspired you will become.
- **Assimilate:** Embed images into your work. Connect unrelated images with colour, unify separate elements with drawn lines and integrate items with paint, texture mediums, wax, sand, etc.
- **Layer:** Add as many layers as your heart desires. If you don't like what you've done, paint it over – it just adds to the layering.

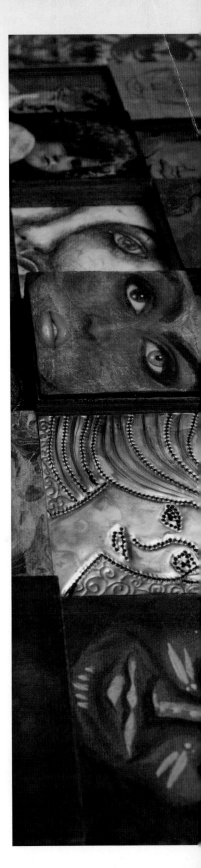

Artful works

Teatime

Tea is a time in which we were perfectly contented with ourselves and one another.

Charles Dickens

Use scrapbooking paper and ink-jet prints of digital photos to make a collage. Add delightful details with scrapbooking embellishments.

Time moves on and we still have a long way to go together. So far we have made it to a record half century of friendship. Not many folks can claim that in the same year as their 50th birthdays. To celebrate ours we took each other out to tea (what else?) at a lovely rose farm where we could combine Monique's favourite pastime of pouring cups that cheer with Angie's penchant for walking in fields of fresh flowers. We had to mark the occasion with our combined passion for photography and food by making this quaint collage depicting tea for two.

You will need

- Support – we used mount board
- Scrapbook kit – ours was a time theme
- Enlarged colour prints (or colour copies) of personal photos
- Extra embellishments – we used stickers, tags, paper flowers, used (dried) tea bags, raffia and cardboard laser-cut clock hands
- Digital camera (optional)
- Glue – repositionable spray adhesive, craft glue, glue gun
- Scissors, craft knife or scalpel
- Brayer
- Clear lacquer spray

1. Assemble all your background papers, pictures and embellishments onto your chosen support and play around with their positioning. Arrange them into a pleasing composition. Use your digital camera to record various options as well as your final decision. This helps when replacing the elements for gluing.

2. Tear or cut prints and copies, depending on the edges required. Cut shapes stand out while torn edges blend more easily. If you tear towards you, the top side of the paper retains the printed colour, while if you tear away from yourself, the unprinted edge (usually white) is revealed as a jagged line. This can emphasize breaks or space between images, but at other times will jar. Painting the edge or chalking it will alleviate this.

3. Glue your main background pieces in position. Roll with a brayer until smooth.

4. Spray the wrong side of your images with the repositionable glue. Allow to dry tacky so that they can be lifted and the position changed if necessary. Set the embellishments in place and check the composition again.

5. When satisfied, stick down and roll images with the brayer. Add further layering with stickers, frames and tags (we used our scrapbook kit). Layer some to cover straight edges or awkward spots.

6. Glue three-dimensional objects with the craft glue or the glue gun.

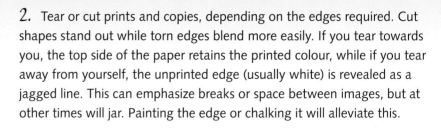

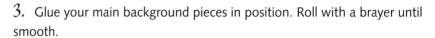

It's a woman thing ...

Display memorabilia and mini collectibles in a printer's tray lined with tinted printed matter and decoupaged vintage pictures.

*It's not junk –
it's a collection.*

Anonymous

In this generation of my family it may be a 'woman thing' to collect, but I inherited the tendency from my dad. My mother is no hoarder. However, I know she will appreciate the feminine aspects of this collection of vintage pictures, religious mementoes, odd souvenirs, jewellery, watches, mini frames and other collectibles. The printer's tray was a gift from a friend's brother who was clearing his office in a large newspaper house. Miranda and I were the lucky recipients of these genuine articles. Craft markets and scrapbooking stores do stock handmade replicas.

Experiment with display themes: match your collections with interesting backgrounds. The little compartments beg to be decorated as individually framed works of art. The backgrounds to my little 'boxes' come from my vast accumulation of printed and written matter: world newspapers with fascinating fonts and scripts, old hoarded letters from my dad, my great-aunt's postcard collection, music and recipe books, dress patterns, old school books, calendars and diaries. I pasted cut-outs from cards, photo-graphs, serviettes and wrapping paper onto these background textures. I had a lot of fun introducing lively reds to warm my theme of women's things before packing the 'shelves' with suitable knick-knacks. You could decorate each 'box' to work individually or as part of a whole, depending on your taste and materials available. I used a vintage theme (you can buy scrap-booking theme packs) but use your imagination. For example, if you are doing one for a person who loves sport, use fixture timetables, match reviews, maps, headlines, advertising and magazine articles that will work with the theme.

You will need

- A printer's tray or replica
- Paper for background decoration
- Ruler (preferably metal) and cutting mat
- Craft knife or rotary cutter
- Paper for decoupage
- Sharp scissors
- Wallpaper glue
- Wood glue
- Medium-sized hog-hair brush and varnish brush
- Acrylic paint in your choice of colour – I used a variety of reds
- Sticky putty
- Double-sided tape – flat and foam backed

1. Measure each compartment carefully. Use the knife, ruler and cutting mat to cut background papers to fit each space snugly. Pre-stretch each piece of paper by pasting on the back and front with wallpaper glue before fitting into place and pasting flat with more glue on the varnish brush. This will avoid wrinkles and bubbles. Try to vary the size and direction of lettering in the printed and written matter.

2. Cut pictures and images from photographs, cards, serviettes, advertisements, etc. with the sharp scissors. Decoupage the cut-outs over the background papers. I also glued dried leaves and chocolate wrappers in place with some wood glue for strength. Think about your theme and try to add items that either illustrate or make some quirky comment about your choice of background, e.g. I added a torn piece of a girls' dress pattern over an advertisement with the word 'Little' predominating. It's touches like this that offer social comment, create a talking point and sustain interest, resulting in an artwork as opposed to a purely decorative piece.

3. I chose red to unify my muddle of backgrounds and decoupaged images as I feel the colour resonates with women. Warm and vibrant – the colour of blood, fire, beautiful flowers and revolution – it evokes passion and playfulness. I love reds all the way from orange through crimson to maroon. Add transparent colour to your paper by drybrushing with acrylics, inks or fabric paints. Make sure the effect is patchy – this adds to the vintage charm.

4. Finally, enjoy selecting and placing suitable (or odd) souvenirs, buttons, bits of jewellery, mini-frames, toys, keys with bits of sticky putty and double-sided tape. Note the mad cow polymer clay pendant alongside the cattle crossing mini roadsign – a relic from a vintage train set. I've used two cameo frames to encapsulate three generations: Grandma, Mom and me.

Solar flare

Plaster board with scraped texture is brought to life with chalk pastels, gel medium and variegated leaf – or cooked copper leaf.

While working on this book, I had a real urge to do something with a sun image and couldn't understand why. I then discovered that there was an unusual amount of solar flare happening at the time, which explained everything. Chalk pastels can be messy and easily smudged and are often avoided as a medium by the inexperienced. When I bought a new box of pastel sticks, I noticed in an insert that one could use baby oil to blend them – this also sounded messy but got me thinking of alternatives. An old favourite – gel medium – provided the answer. Matte medium and other similar products work too, as well as gesso, though this makes the colours lighter and more pastel. I re-used an old canvas in the process too.

You will need

- Canvas or other support
- Plaster of Paris
- Sieve
- Cold glue
- Scrapers
- Soft chalk pastels – I bought a small mixed box
- Gel medium
- Medium and large paintbrushes
- Variegated or copper leaf
- Tacky glue or metal leaf size

1. Paint the canvas liberally with glue. Lie flat, and before it dries, sieve plaster of Paris over it in a thick layer. Allow to stand for an hour or two. Tip up, allowing the excess plaster powder to fall away. Brush away all the excess with a large brush and gather this together for another project.

2. Scratch into the layer of plaster with scrapers to create a simple texture.

3. Draw your image in chalk pastel. At this stage it will seem light and uninteresting and all the chalk marks will show. I used an ochre, red oxide, dark grey combination in the frame area and a pink, red, orange combination in the sun. The background 'sky' area was made up of turquoise and a flesh colour.

4. Dip the smaller brush into the gel medium and work over the pastel. It is important to clean your brush off often, or the image will appear very muddy. Remember your journal – this is a golden opportunity to create a background page for something else. The gel will blend the pastel and seal it at the same time, allowing you to work over it as you wish. Allow to dry or speed up the drying time with a hairdryer.

5. Scratch again to create more texture, especially in the sun area.

6. Draw with pastel again, using the same colours. This layering adds depth and makes the colours richer. Repeat the gel painting process.

7. Add another layer to darken your image still further with more focus in the sun. Repeat the gel painting process.

8. Add variegated metal leaf in irregular strips. Paint the area you wish to cover with tacky glue or metal leaf size. Allow to dry tacky and then carefully apply the leaf film. Use baby powder on your hands so that it doesn't stick. I couldn't find variegated leaf at the time, so I 'cooked' some copper leaf in the oven to achieve a similar effect (180°C for about 5 minutes between two sheets of non-stick paper).

9. I added a line to the left and under each strip of metal leaf with dark grey chalk pastel. This was also blended with gel medium and left to dry. It added a shadow line, giving the image more depth.

Family silver

Family faces are magic mirrors: looking at people who belong to us, we see the past, present, and future.

Gail Lumet Buckley

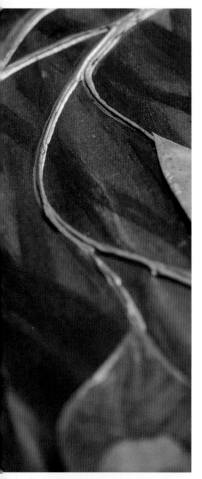

Painted paper and acrylic glazes add depth and texture to a dark board.

This family tree is one-sided and only shows my immediate family on its leaves – my mother and father, my brother and I, and our children. If I were to go further I would not be able to find space on this board for all the faces requiring leaves. I decided to call it family silver as, although I did not inherit any real silver, I have my worth and dependence in the 'magic mirror' faces of my past, present and future. Try working from a dark background to create your own family tree in the shadowy family forest of generations.

You will need

- Acrylic paints
- Water
- Wood glue or podge
- Hog-hair brushes, old toothbrushes, fresh strong-veined leaves, stamps
- Waste copy paper from your printer – preferably printed on one side only
- Scissors
- Dark mountboard
- Chalk
- Texture paste
- Palette knife
- Metallic pens – I used gel and felt-tip markers in silver and gold
- Silver fabric paint liner
- Ink-jet copies of family photos – one thumbnail image for each member
- Wax crayons
- Double-sided tape

1. Make acrylic glazes by watering down acrylic paints to a runny consistency. Add a tiny dab of wood glue or podge before pouring, dripping, spattering and stamping the glazes onto the copy paper using brushes, toothbrushes, real leaves and stamps as tools. Allow to dry and repeat the process on the printed side so that all the paper is painted on both sides. Cut leaf shapes from these decorated sheets of paper. I used simple gum leaf shapes for my design.

2. Chalk a simple tree in the foreground on one side of a piece of charcoal or navy mountboard. Use the palette knife to spread texture paste thinly up the tree shape. Tear printed copy paper into thin strips and stick these vertically into the texture paste to resemble bark. Paint thinner trunk and branch shapes in podge or woodglue onto the board next to the large tree shape. These will dry clear, shinier and darker than the mountboard colour and appear as shadowy trees behind the main family tree.

3. Mix more purple, pink, grey and brown glazes and allow to run down the main tree. Use a brush to colour in the background trees with the grey and brown glazes, defining the tree shapes and the negative spaces between them. Add more branch detail towards the top of the picture.

4. Use the metallic gel pens to write in the family members' names and dates on the main trunk and subsidiary branches. I wrote my parents in the main trunk and my brother and me and our partners on the other branches.

5. Chalk in fine twig lines and leaves sweeping across the main tree. I worked out how many branches and leaves were required to represent my family and drew a small sketch to work from.

6. Outline the twigs only with silver fabric liner. Don't stress if the lines are a bit rough or wonky – this adds to the twiggy effect. Allow the liner to dry before proceeding.

7. Tear the individual faces from the ink-jet prints. Paste each one on a cut leaf with podge and allow to dry. Decide on a pleasing arrangement of leaves at the end of each twig line and mark the position with chalk.

8. Remove the leaves and draw and rub more texture on the trunk and background with red, brown, pink and grey wax crayons. Add silver lines with the felt marker to the main tree as well as the edges of each leaf allowing them to stand out from the background.

9. Place each leaf in its position with a small strip of double-sided tape so that it is able to curl slightly off the backing board, creating a three-dimensional effect.

Capsicum

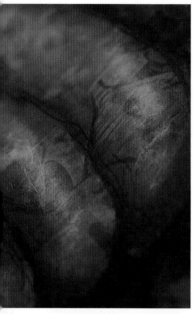

Texture and colour backgrounds with torn painted paper. Add shading and highlighting with complementary acrylic colours.

One of my favourite things to do when I lack inspiration is to mess on paper. This provides lots of background paper for all sorts of projects when I need them and they are wonderful for collages. For this project, I assembled various pieces of paper with similar colours and feel and used them as a background for this painting. If you have a fear of the white page, this is an inspiring way to start a painting. If the colours are a bit bright, you can always lighten the whole piece with gesso or white paint before you begin. My peppers *are* bright, but I love them – like Betsy in 'the Simpson' who reckons it's all about little substitutions: "If you want to eat something, eat a bell pepper. Crave something sweet? Eat a bell pepper. Want a beer? Bell pepper."

You will need

- Support – I used a canvas board
- Painted paper – recycled. Or use colourful magazine paper
- Glue
- Brayer
- Acrylic paint in yellow, variety of reds, viridian (phthalo green) and white
- Paintbrushes
- Charcoal pencil
- Fixative

1. Tear the paper into irregular shapes and glue to the support. Make sure the edges are well glued. Use a brayer to stick the paper down securely and to remove any air bubbles.

2. Draw the peppers onto the paper in pencil or chalk. I used pencil lines for the effect they create as a resist to the charcoal used later on.

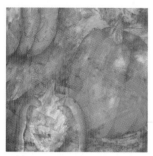

3. Using washes of red and green, paint around the peppers to darken the background slightly. You still want the paper to show through. Make sure any white from the torn paper is coloured.

4. Paint the peppers using green and yellow on one, a variety of reds on another and red and yellow on the third. Make various shades of green by mixing viridian with yellow and/or red. Peppers are simple shapes and easy to paint by darkening along the edges and working lighter towards the top centre of each bulbous area. The pepper that is cut in half has darker shading on either side of the seed area.

5. Highlight the bulbous areas still more by drybrushing with white. The central seed area of the green cut pepper is also drybrushed. The seeds are filled in lightly with white and then a thin, darker green stripe painted to one side to make them appear more three-dimensional.

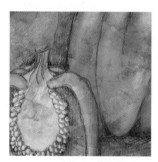

6. Charcoal provides the finishing touch: 'scribble' around each of the peppers creating a rough outline for effect. Finish off the painting by writing 'Capsicum' in different areas for added texture.

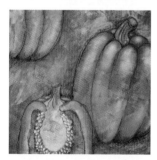

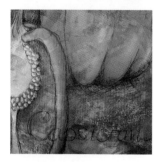

Fresh fruit

Combine paper rubbings, corrugated board, wire and paint to create the layered effects of this fruity work.

In a way, this is a portrait of the pair of us. When we decided which fruit to paint, these two came top of the list as one of us is an apple, the other a pear.

Not the easiest medium to work on, aluminium foil reflects light like no other. You could substitute the foil with tissue paper for an equally crinkled effect, though it won't of course reflect the luminosity of these rich reds. I have made my paintings quite moody; you can make yours lighter, brighter and more colourful if you like, by using different colours.

You will need

- Support – I used primed wooden blocks
- Wire
- Pliers
- Corrugated board
- Craft knife
- Aluminium foil or tissue paper
- Artists' spray fixative if painting on foil
- Glue and glue in a liner bottle – I used stencil glue
- Liner bottle
- Painted paper – recycled. Make lots of random textures using the same colours as you intend for the final painting
- Wax crayons – I used blue and red
- Acrylic paint: I used Payne's grey, cobalt blue, cadmium red, burnt sienna. For the acrylic paint you can substitute glass paint (acetone is the solvent) or alcohol inks (use ammonia as the solvent)
- Soft paintbrushes
- Hake brush
- Lacquer spray

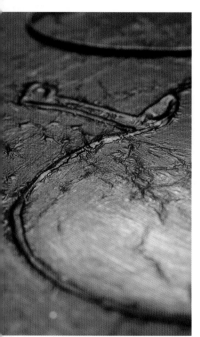

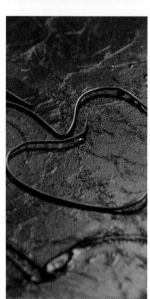

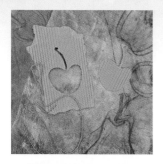

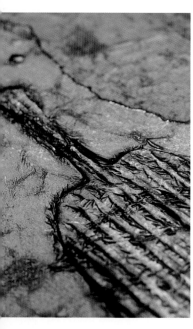

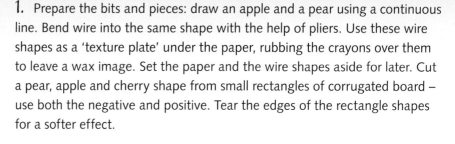

1. Prepare the bits and pieces: draw an apple and a pear using a continuous line. Bend wire into the same shape with the help of pliers. Use these wire shapes as a 'texture plate' under the paper, rubbing the crayons over them to leave a wax image. Set the paper and the wire shapes aside for later. Cut a pear, apple and cherry shape from small rectangles of corrugated board – use both the negative and positive. Tear the edges of the rectangle shapes for a softer effect.

2. Using the bits and pieces, prepare the board. Draw a pear and a section of a pear cut in half onto the board in pencil – do the same for the apple. Using a liner bottle filled with glue, draw over the lines, creating a raised effect. You could use any other paint medium in a liner bottle that will stay raised. Glue one negative and one positive fruit shape onto the board. Brayer to make sure they are well glued.

3. When the raised glue lines have dried tacky, paint glue all over, including onto the corrugated shapes, and stick a sheet of foil to it. Make the foil as flat as possible, using a brayer.

4. Tear around the wax rubbings on the painted paper and stick where required on the foil. You can add small bits of paper here and there for extra colour and texture.

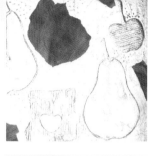

5. Taking a cue from the paper, paint the foil using the same colours and a large, flat brush. To blend and soften the brush marks, use a hake brush. Work as quickly as you can: working into dry paint will lift it. If you don't like what you've painted, spray the work with water, wipe off and start again. When you're happy with the effect and the paint is dry, spray with fixative and leave to dry.

6. Add the dark colours (blue and Payne's gray) around the shapes to enhance their brighter colours. This second layer of paint is easier to apply.

7. When you're happy with your painting, spray with lacquer spray and glue the wire shapes into position.

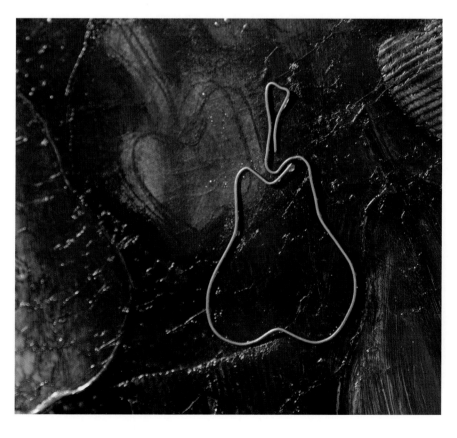

List the leaves

Confront your fears, list them, get to know them, and only then will you be able to put them aside and move ahead.

Jerry Gillies

Decoupaging with dried leaves, foiling, shellac and pewter embossing.

When planning ideas, workloads and schedules I tend to 'leave the lists' to my beloved co-author, so I decided to surprise her here with this project called 'list the leaves' as a canny twist as well as a mixed media procedure list. You can make up your own procedure list for yourself or for a painting group. If you are ever stuck for ideas, this is fun to do and a good way of channelling ideas, processes and pieces into a single creative outcome.

I have a large collection of bits and bobs as well as experience of techniques to use, but groups can organise these as a lucky draw. Brain storm briefly and write a list of suggested mixed media and techniques. Cut the list into as many items as there are members of your group. Each draws one from the pool and brings enough relevant materials and tools to share. Group work is much more stimulating and varied with exciting and creative results as each member encourages development of the other. Decide on the order of techniques you will follow and tick each item off the list as you go – plan to glue and write your list into the final collage.

I managed to work leaves into my list. If you would like to try copying my efforts you will not get the same results, but ...

You will need

- **Techniques list:** Mine incorporated pasting, drybrushing, tearing, leafing, stamping, painting, foiling, printing, shellac varnishing, pewter embossing
- **Tools list:** Varnish brushes, brayer, stamps, pewter ball tool for embossing (or an old crochet hook and dry ballpoint pens), sheet of glass, clean paper, credit card
- **Tackle list:** Canvas supports (I recycled old rejected acrylic paintings by painting them with white acrylic first), real leaves (dried for texture and fresh for leaf prints and rubbings – I used beautiful castor oil leaves but any strongly veined leaf will do nicely – you could also incorporate skeleton leaves), leaves from letters, books and magazines (about leaves), metal leaf (I used gold and silver), leaf stamps, acrylic gel medium, white acrylic paint, gold paint stick, turpentine (as solvent), grey/black printing ink, shellac, denatured alcohol (methylated spirits), metallic fibre-tip pens,

large fibre-tip glue pen, foil, 3D metal leaves (bought or created using pewter or aluminium – coffee can lids or seals are wonderful (for recycling), silicone glue

1. Paste the smooth side of your dried leaves with gel medium and glue these face down randomly to the canvas. Use more gel medium on the veined side to smooth the leaves down well using a varnish brush. Work out any air bubbles at the same time. Leave to dry. (I decided to use a second canvas as I had enough dried leaves and the composition would be more interesting.)

2. Drybrush the canvases all over with white acrylic. The leaf veins will stand out and show their texture as the layers of drybrushing increase. Stop before you blot out the veins in a snowy field of white paint.

3. Tear the paper leaves from books and magazines – I found old advertisements for castor oil which were a nice touch – and glue them randomly to the canvases as well, with the gel and brush. Allow to dry.

4. Paste gel medium thinly in random patches over the leaves and gaps. While still wet, cover lightly with metal leaf. Use a dry varnish brush to pat the leaf down onto the gel medium. Do not rub. Allow to dry for at least an hour and then gently rub off excess metal leaf.

5. Stamp dark grey leaves in patches over sections of both canvases. Stamp several times off one inking so that you get lighter prints. Re-ink the stamp with gold ink and stamp over and around the grey leaves.

6. Drybrush more white over the stamping to soften and blend the images into the background. Rub a little gold paint stick here and there and soften by blending with a little turps.

7. At this point I rotated the canvases to decide which way they would group together best.

8. The combinations were becoming dull so I decided to tear up my original list and incorporate it. Each piece was pasted in place with more gel medium.

9. Provide some textural contrast by leaf printing. Ink the plate of glass and press flattened fresh leaves into the ink. Place leaves in position on the canvas, cover with clean paper and roll lightly with the brayer to print vein patterns over and between the actual leaves.

10. Shellac flakes dissolved in denatured alcohol make a lovely gold varnish which dries quickly. Paint this around and between the edges of the original pasted leaves, allowing them to show up against the varnish.

11. Scribble some writing – I wrote my listed objects – down the side of both canvases using gold and silver fibre-tip markers.

12. Brush the glue pen lightly over the surface relief of the veins and textures on the canvases. Wait until the glue dries tacky and then foil these as highlights. This adds a lively sparkle particularly when viewing the work from the side as the foiled areas catch the light.

13. Add 3D pewter leaves for the finishing touch. These are simple to make: trace around small leaves onto the wrong side of your pewter and cut out each shape. Draw the main vein lines on the wrong side of each leaf using a pencil. Lightly indent finer lines and toothed edges using a darning needle. Cover each pewter leaf on the wrong (indented) side with silicone glue using a credit card. Press them into place, wrapping some carefully over the boxed edges of the canvases where necessary. Wipe off the excess glue before leaving them to dry for a few hours.

Note: I could have added patina to the pewter to darken it and then polished the leaves leaving the darkened areas in the spaces between the veins, but I felt they needed to be shiny so left them as they were. The final effect is as gently muddled and pictorial as lists become in my head.

Fiftea

Use unusual and related elements: pasted tea bags, writing texture, shaded painting with metal leaf to highlight the tea theme.

Fifty tea bags bear testimony to our combined friendship and Penny's passion for consuming constant cups of her best brew. Husband Paul flew all her friends to her for a fantastic surprise party. We had to make her something which would work together although we come from opposite sides of the country – and the theme was indisputable. To honour her mathematical and scientific talents as well as her age, we arranged our works as squares: five to the power of two, times two, with written quotations on the tea bags – fiftea in all. We added a further ten plain bags representing a table cloth on which to rest her brimming cup.

Come and share a pot of tea, my home is warm and my friendship's free.

Emilie Barnes

You will need

- Drink lots of tea; dry 50 tea bags and divest them of their treasure – keep the leaves for another project)
- Support – we used two blocks made from MDF
- Wood glue (watered down 2:1)
- HB pencil
- Brayer
- White, burnt sienna and burnt umber acrylic paint
- Medium and fine brushes
- Feather
- Variegated metal leaf
- Tacky glue or gilding milk
- Clear lacquer

1. Iron the teabags to flatten them. Arrange them in a pleasing combination of light and dark checkerboard pattern. Apply wood glue to the supports and position the bags overlapping slightly. Roll smooth with the brayer. When dry, write quotes on them in pencil and then seal with a diluted wash of wood glue to prevent the pencil from smudging.

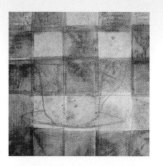

2. Draw in the cup, saucer and teapot shapes. Make sure the spout lines up with the centre of the cup.

3. Paint the cup, saucer and teapot white. Shade with burnt sienna and umber.

4. Apply gilding milk or glue in a decorative pattern to the cup, saucer and teapot with a fine brush. Leave to dry tacky. Apply metal leaf and dust off excess with a soft brush.

5. Dip the feather into a watered down mix of burnt sienna and white. Softly drag the feather in a twirling line between the spout and the centre of the cup. Repeat this a few times to simulate liquid tea being poured. Highlight the twirls here and there with metal leaf for a hint of heat. Spray the finished work with clear lacquer to seal.

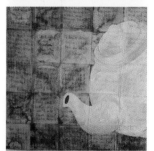

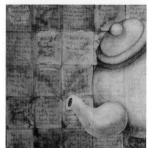

Adinkra apology

Stencil with tea, monoprint some stylish symbols, decoupage serviettes and embellish the collage with found natural objects.

Sometimes I feel I spend my life making mistakes, blunders and slip-ups, resulting in misunderstanding and unhappiness for others – and myself. My slip-ups are usually not deliberate, but caused by my poor memory or distracted (overloaded) brain. Nevertheless, others get hurt and disappointed through my lapses, so I spend much time apologising, trying to rebuild connections, with new resolutions to learn from my mistakes.

The Sankofa Adinkra symbol really speaks to me. It literally translates as "return and retrieve" but the deeper meaning is that there is nothing to be ashamed of with learning from hindsight. Sankofa expresses the wisdom and knowledge we carry from our past actions as we progress. Various images depict a mythical bird that flies forward with its head turned backwards and also a heart shape. Mistakes can be rectified with heart (love and courage) and humility.

I made this for Penny whom I hurt by forgetting to let her know I was not coming to stay with her ... until it was too late. I now have to remember to read my diary daily – and where I put it! To make a collage in this style ...

You will need

- A few sheets of A4 copy paper – I used some dyed with coffee to age them
- Large black felt marker with bullet tip
- Paper printed with symbols
- Cutter and mat
- Sheet of handmade paper
- Stencil brush
- Gel medium
- 2 used dry teabags
- Printing inks in your choice of colours – I used brown and black
- Printing plate (slightly larger than A5 size) – a sheet of Perspex or glass works well

- Brayer and rolling pin
- Paper serviette in style and colours which work with your theme
- Sharp scissors
- Wallpaper glue
- Soft varnish brush
- Found objects: shells, bits of rust, beads, bottle caps
- Texture paste
- Painting palette knife
- Quills – I found these on the road where a porcupine had been run over (I don't buy quills as too many animals are killed deliberately to satisfy the market need)
- Large sewing needle and strong, coloured thread

1. Write Sankofa with the black marker and cut out the lettering with a sharp cutter on the mat. Position on the handmade paper and stencil the lettering with gel medium. Slit open the tea bags and shake dried tea over the gel medium lettering and leave to dry. Shake off excess tea leaves revealing your tea 'flocking'. Reserve empty tea bags.

2. Cut the Sankofa symbol shapes from the printed paper very carefully. Roll brown ink onto the printing plate and then position the Sankofa shapes onto the wet ink. Re-roll the printing plate very carefully with black ink. The second inking will pull up some of the brown ink in patches around the stencil, cut-out shapes. Fold a sheet of A4 paper (I used a coffee-dyed sheet) into A5 size and place onto the printing plate. Rub gently all over with your hands and then with the rolling pin. Lift the print to reveal the stencil shape on a mottled brown and black background. Lay the print aside. Use the needle point to lift the stencil shapes and put them somewhere to dry.

3. Create ghost images by using the blank side of the folded piece face down on the printing plate. Cover with a clean piece of paper and rub with your hands and roll with the rolling pin again. Lift the print and use a fresh piece of paper to print ghost images until the ink is used up. Choose the prints you like best and cut or tear two into A5-size pieces.

4. Cut shapes or 'frames' from the serviette and use the needle point to separate layers of backing tissue from the printed tissue. Arrange printed tissue cuts, flattened empty tea bags and paper prints onto the handmade paper in a pleasing composition. Glue the pieces in position with the varnish brush using wallpaper glue under and on top of the pieces. The serviette tissue and tea bags will 'melt' effortlessly into the texture of the handmade paper; the copy paper will need a bit of gentle rubbing to do the same.

5. Arrange found objects to enhance the composition and glue into place using texture paste and the palette knife. Use gel medium to glue the cut and printed stencil shapes into position as well.

6. I used quills to link the blocky areas and serviette tissue frames because the colours and lines worked so well against the textures. As they would have been difficult to glue, I decided to stitch them in place with strong coloured thread using the large needle. Twigs and leaves as well as thin bits of driftwood can all be attached in this way.

Transforming tricks

Quirky collage using a magazine challenge, various decoupage techniques and some extra tips.

The aim of this collage was to create a visual story in the altered-image genre using pictures cut from one magazine and collaged onto a background of mixed scrap papers. This is an exciting challenge for teachers to inspire enthusiasm for quirky expression in their classes. For those concerned with not being able to draw accurately, this becomes great fun, freeing the imagination to run riot and the hands to experiment with colour and composition, cut, glue, copy over lines, and scribble details and shadows.

Try setting your own challenge. I used a home and decor magazine and was really surprised at the wealth of images in the advertising as well as the articles. It enabled me to create this delightful scene of two cats chatting over a cuppa. I found the caption 'Transforming tricks' in the same magazine – it seemed perfect for this exercise as a whole.

The two cats, obviously two friends, symbolise Monique and me. Our symbols being the aardvark and chameleon begged to be included as I had pounced gleefully on a chameleon in the magazine. However, the aardvark had me stumped. No magazine had a picture of one. So I decided that challenges are there to be challenged: I 'cheated' and printed the aardvark. My motto is that everyone should bend rules a little – it saves us from becoming rigid.

You will need

- Mount board or backing card (cut up an old cereal box)
- Scrap papers for pasting a background collage – I used a fishy serviette, crepe paper, mottled wallpaper and torn pages of an old book
- Wallpaper glue
- Varnish brush
- Acrylic glazes
- One magazine – choose one with a wide range of pictures
- Scissors – I used embroidery scissors
- Hog-hair brushes in various sizes
- Black fine line markers
- 3D embellishments – I used a feather and a metal fish charm
- Liquid chalk for antiquing

sea

Tea

TRANSFORMING TRICKS

1. Start by flipping through your magazine and roughly cutting out images that appeal to you. Assemble these on your chosen size of mount board and play around with a composition. Now go carefully through the magazine again and cut out any other images and words that will work with your story. Discard others and continue playing with the composition. The pre-dominance of cats, teacups and fish suggested spelling out Sea A Tea spells cat (my original title). The quirky underwater scene just developed easily after that. I added elements that would cover gaps and awkward cutting, all the while adding to the symbolism and fun.

2. Once I knew where the lampshade would illumine my underwater scene I could decide how to design the backdrop using crepe paper, wallpaper and torn paper. The colours of my cut-outs as well as the sea and lampshade determined the blue, yellow and greens. I washed the crepe paper with blue along the grain and added yellow to the leftover blue paint to tone a green wash for the torn page 'carpeting'.

3. Once the backdrop was dry I cut the fish carefully from the paper serviette, separating the layers after the fish were cut perfectly. The 'ghost' images left from the cut were put to one side. I pasted the fish swimming in the blue crepe paper sea with wallpaper glue and the soft varnish brush. The fish blended neatly into the crepe paper.

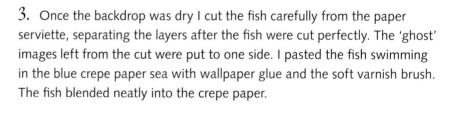

4. The ghost fish images were then pasted onto the yellow-green mottled wallpaper to represent almost transparent fish, swimming through the background of light, cast by the lampshade.

5. The main features of my story were pasted in at this point. I used wallpaper glue so that it makes it easier to reposition elements – simply lift with a damp brush. Other glues bond too quickly and will tear the paper.

6. At this stage I began to unify the elements into one picture by outlining each in a sketchy fashion with the fine line marker. It was also time to take stock of the composition and work out where more balance was required and where I might fit a few more irresistible images to deepen the 'plot' and give the story added quirks. For example: Monique is a lady who wears many hats so I was delighted to find this neat pile advertising a fashion article.

7. Some final additions and scribbling gave more cohesion to the story overall. I added the finishing touch with a little rub from a scrapbooker's antiquing liquid 'chalk' pad.

Bene dominum venisti

Introducing texture paste as an integrating medium and stencilling to enhance collage and painting.

I love the shapes of plants when they have gone to seed. The textures and patterns are seemingly endless. An elderly uncle in Holland was often in the habit of sending seeds and other odd things to me through the post (including the last grape of the season wrapped in foil) – all probably quite illegal. So, a copy of a letter accompanying such a *cadeau*, seemed the right thing to add to this collaged background, together with printouts of dictionary definitions of seeds and texture paste. The final touch to this painting of dandelions was added with stencils.

You will need

- Support – I used a canvas block
- Photocopies or printouts of images and writing
- Glue
- Brayer
- Texture paste
- Palette knife
- Acrylic paint – Payne's grey, cerulean blue, yellow ochre, deep rose and white
- Paintbrushes including a hake brush and a very fine watercolour brush
- Chalk
- Stencils – curls and lettering
- Stencil brush or sponge

1. Tear the edges of the copies to the size and shapes you need for your composition. Stick down with glue, taking care to glue to the very edges of the paper. Brayer over the paper to make sure it is stuck well and that all the air bubbles are released.

2. Add texture paste with a palette knife so that it covers the edges of the torn paper in most places. This will dry white, though it will still be somewhat transparent.

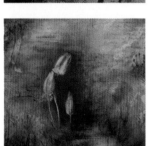

3. Paint a thin patchy wash of blue, ochre, Payne's grey and white: thin the paint down with a little water. Use the white sparingly as this makes the colours appear chalky. Soften and blend with a hake brush. Repeat this until you are happy with the saturation of colour.

4. Add more Payne's grey around the dark copy so that the edges appear less harsh and blend into the rest of the picture.

5. Draw the dandelions in chalk to check their size and placement. A composition works best when the focal point intersects the division of thirds. In other words, mentally divide the support into three, vertically and horizontally, resulting in a grid. Any one of the intersecting points can be a focal area.

6. With the thin watercolour brush, paint the dandelions white. For the best 'tapered' effect, paint each line from the centre out.

7. Add form and shadows to the dandelion with a dirty pink – make this with rose and Payne's grey. You can also add some dark green shadow lines made with Payne's grey, blue and ochre.

8. Add further layered detail with the stencils of words and curls using Payne's grey. Use a stencil brush or sponge but either way, do it lightly. If you paint them in too solidly (too harsh for this picture), spray them quickly and dab the excess paint off. Leave to dry.

9. Drybrush the texture with white. Less is more with this technique – you just want to touch the edges of the texture to highlight the effect.

Play housey housey with me

Introducing negative mono-printing, enhanced with vibrant acrylic inks and textural stamping.

Somewhere inside all of us is a little fantasy. Armed with many photographs upon returning from an overseas trip, I was struck by how many buildings I'd captured. When I examined them closely I realised I'd focused on particular architectural details and that the turrets looked just like fairy houses – so here we are, with my interpretation. Painted on tags, my avenue of quirky houses is coloured in bright acrylic inks. This was a golden opportunity to practise colour mixing as I only used the primaries. The tracing process is a little different too, adding texture of its own.

You will need

- Manila tags or other support
- Papers to glue on: I used newspaper, a map, a list, a piece of dress pattern, graph paper, house plans and sheet music – none of which will be that apparent once you've finished, but all add to the effect.
- Glue
- Gesso
- Burnt sienna and black acrylic paint
- Acrylic retarder
- Good quality tracing paper
- Brayer
- Pencil
- Acrylic ink – just the primaries will do: yellow, magenta and cyan
- Watercolour brushes
- Small stamps (optional)
- Ribbon or string to finish off (optional)

1. My Manila tags came in sets of four, so I left them that way to begin with, though it doesn't really matter. Glue various bits of paper to the tags, allowing some to encroach onto the next tag.

2. Paint lightly with gesso or white paint, allowing the various textures of print to show through.

3. Paint with a thin wash of burnt sienna – the paint should appear quite patchy: darker at the top and the bottom. When dry, separate the tags – you may need to cut them if the paper has been glued across two.

4. Trace all the houses onto separate pieces of tracing paper.

5. Mix a little acrylic retarder with the black acrylic paint. This extends the working time of the paint. Work on one house at a time: brayer a thin layer of the black acrylic mix onto the back of the tracing paper. Turn this onto a tag and retrace along the lines creating a 'negative tracing' effect. You will be left with an impression of the house and the background will be a little marked with the paint, adding an aged effect.

6. Keep the negative tracings – they can be used in another project. Use milky pens and chalks to colour them.

7. Have fun mixing as many colours as you can from the three primary inks. (Magenta and yellow make orange; magenta and blue make purple. Mix blue and yellow for green.) Paint the houses, blending a variety of shades and tones for effect.

8. To create a sky effect, thin down a little blue ink and paint in a patchy way at the top of each tag, blending to nothing as you come down the tag. A small hake brush is very useful for this. Paint green more definitely at the bottom for the land.

9. Taking your cue from the most dominant colour on the house, stamp small motifs on the house and the background to create a quirky texture.

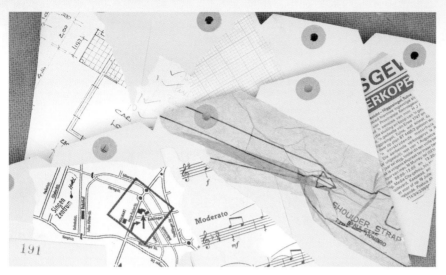

Serenity

3D wallpaper and stamping add textural dimension to a background collage of scrapbooking, or other pre-printed paper, for this softly shaded portrait.

I am not a scrapbooker though I must admit that there are loads of wonderful papers just itching to be incorporated into a mixed-media painting. I also came across this paintable embossed wallpaper, which matched the circle theme perfectly and added an additional textural effect. There are beautiful, more complicated, patterned wallpapers which would be great on other projects. I have picked up on the colours of the paper and used a very limited palette. With this small collection of colours one can create many variations. This iconic lady of mine makes other appearances, in different guises, in Smart Art and Simply Fabulous Fabric.

You will need

- Support
- Paper – I used scrapbooking sheets and painted scrap paper. Gift wrap is another option
- Paintable wallpaper
- Gesso
- Paintbrushes
- Acrylic paint – I matched colours from the paper: burnt sienna, red oxide, hookers green and yellow ochre: you may have a different palette
- Stamps or stencils (optional); you could add to the circle theme by printing with bubble wrap
- Sandpaper

1. Tear a section of paintable wallpaper, (about one third of the width of the canvas) and glue down the length of the canvas on the right. Tear around the edges of the scrapbooking paper and glue those close together on the left. It is better to have torn edges as very straight edges are distracting and more difficult to integrate.

2. Paint white gesso in the vague area where you will paint the head. Don't worry if you still see through to the pattern of the paper.

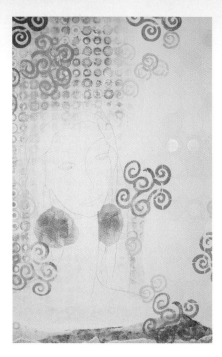

3. Draw the head in lightly with pencil. Add more paper to the earring and dress areas and paint lightly with gesso.

4. Using stamps of your choice, print random patterns over the painting in various colours – though not too dark. Mix white into the colours if necessary. You may go over the head in one or two places, for added effect.

5. Paint thin washes of burnt sienna, red oxide and hookers green with a little white around the lady to colour the wallpaper, blending into the scrapbooking paper. Give the dress a light wash of red oxide. Here again, it is desirable to see the pattern of the papers through the paint. If you paint too thickly, spray the paint and blot off with waste paper – the start of another project.

6. To create extra texture you may want to sand the background lightly to reveal the gesso through the colours.

7. Shade around your lady again with washes in the same colours. Paint the hair in thicker paint in the same combination, adding yellow ochre to highlight some areas. Add green to the red to create shadows. Drybrush over the face and neck as you're going along, creating a skin tone.

8. Add definition to the face and other skin areas with a drybrush mix of burnt sienna, Indian red and (to make the dark colour) green again. Paint around the edges of the face, to the right of the nose and chin. Also, under the chin, on each side of the neck and on the right of the neck where it meets the body. Paint the eyes green and add a little lipstick with red oxide, leaving a slightly lighter patch in the centre of the bottom lip. Give your lady some eyebrows too.

9. The darker drybrush shading around the edges of the lady may seem a little harsh so drybrush with white in the centre of each cheek, the forehead and down the centre right of the neck. Paint the earrings with the same combination of colours, accenting with red oxide. Paint a chain to attach them to the ears using red oxide and yellow ochre and a touch of white. I felt my background was a bit dark so I lightened it with a wash of white, blotting it as I went along.

Reliquary for a wreck

Antiquities are history defaced, or some remnants of history which have casually escaped the shipwreck of time.

Francis Bacon

Create an antique, metal-leafed reliquary from corrugated cardboard, copper paint, stamps and DIY self-hardening clay.

The Portuguese galleon Sacramento was on her maiden voyage from India to Portugal in 1647 when she was wrecked off the coast of Port Elizabeth. I can see the wreck site from my bedroom window and on stormy nights imagine this little old ship breaking up in the waves, scattering her cargo on the sea bed. Our family lived in the village of Schoenmakerskop from where the salvage operation was directed when the wreck was discovered in 1976. As a young girl I had played in the rock pools and as a teenager searched for shells to string into necklaces. In one rock pool I found an ancient coin (a piece of eight) and a few bits of coppery brass and chain, green with verdigris and encrusted with coral growths. I've held onto these wreck relics over the years and decided that the current craze for mixed-media vintage reliquaries would be ideal to showcase my findings. I made my own reliquary from an old cardboard box and some leftover copper paint from a project for our Smart Art book. It had blackened with time but worked its verdigris wonder when the patina was applied. You could use any paint or decoupaged paper to decorate your own particular relics.

You will need

- Corrugated cardboard box
- Craft knife and cutting mat
- Strong scissors
- Gummed brown paper tape
- Cotton fabric strip
- Wood glue
- Varnish brush
- Gold spray-painted newspaper
- Self-hardening clay – DIY recipe ratio: 1 teaspoon wood glue kneaded well with 1 crustless slice of white bread
- Stamps – I used vintage angel wings and Phillips screw heads
- Masking tape
- Brown oxide paint
- Copper paint

- Verdigris patina
- Burnt umber acrylic paint
- Variegated metal leaf
- Stencil glue
- Copper adhesive tape
- Relics and background picture: I printed a picture of the galleon on watercolour paper and antiqued the edges with liquid chalk
- Double-sided tape
- Sticky putty
- Sealing wax and matches
- Embellishments – I used antique carved bonefish buttons

1. Cut two matching cardboard backs and four side flaps from the corrugated cardboard box. Cut a 'window' as a frame for your relics in one of the backs. Cover two of the side flaps with some gold-painted newspaper. Use leftover pieces of cardboard to decorate the window piece and the other two side flaps with extra raised pieces. Glue securely using wood glue. Cover these side flaps with small torn strips of gummed brown paper tape. Sandwich brown paper and gold paper-covered side flaps on either side of the plain, flat back piece with the strip of cotton fabric. Cut a piece of gold-painted newspaper slightly larger than the window space and paste in position over the fabric so that it will form a background for the window piece.

2. Cover the window piece with more torn gummed paper tape and glue it over the flat back piece with more wood glue. The reliquary is now assembled and when the glue is set, it is ready to decorate.

3. Roll a few thin 'sausages' of 'clay'. Paste wood glue over the raised areas and press the clay rolls around them, moulding it to smooth the edges. Impress with Phillips screw heads making a little cross pattern. Press more clay to cover the cut-out shapes on the side flaps. Impress the angel wings or other stamps into the clay. If you leave this clay at least 4mm thick it will crack very satisfyingly into the design lines as it dries.

4. Mask off the gold paper areas with masking tape and paint the entire reliquary with copper paint and allow to dry.

5. Paint verdigris patina over the copper paint and wait for the lovely green to appear. This takes only a few hours to develop.

6. Stamp the angel wings with burnt umber acrylic onto the gold paper-covered side flaps. Cut copper tape to frame the window space. Apply stencil glue to the raised areas with the varnish brush. Wash the brush immediately. Apply variegated leaf, wait for half an hour and brush off excess skewings.

7. Position relics and stick into the window space with the putty, sealing wax and double-sided tape. Add the chain or some form of closing tie to the front of the reliquary. Decorate with the bone buttons.

 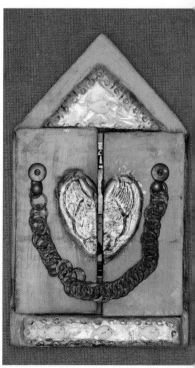

Old friends

Old friends, sat on a park bench like bookends. Can you imagine us years from today sharing a park bench quietly? How terribly strange to be fifty. Memory brushes the same years, silently sharing the same careers.

Paul Simon (with a little artistic licence)

Negative and positive stencilling, engraving, clouding and oil rubbing combine for interesting textural effects.

When we were much younger, Angie and I listened to Simon and Garfunkel, "Old friends" being one of our favourites. Little did we think then that we would be the bookends to our own books. When time came to make a birthday card for Angie, I couldn't resist adding the words of the song – albeit with a few changes. The fish and bird images are those that we each seem drawn to and use most often.

You will need

- Support – I used black mount board. Paint the back with any acrylic paint to stop it from curling at a later stage
- Crack filler with a little glue added
- Credit card
- Stencils – fish and negative bird shapes
- Kebab stick or nail
- Acrylic paint in burnt sienna, viridian, blue and white
- Paintbrushes
- Oil paint in Payne's grey
- Resin-based oil medium
- Clean, soft cloth
- Turpentine to clean oil paintbrush
- Hairdryer – optional

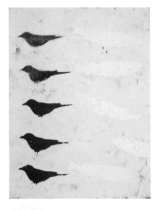

1. Place the small bird stencil negative onto the mount board and scrape around it with crack filler. There is no need to be too smooth as it is the texture that makes this project. Repeat this for as many bird images as you wish to have – I did five.

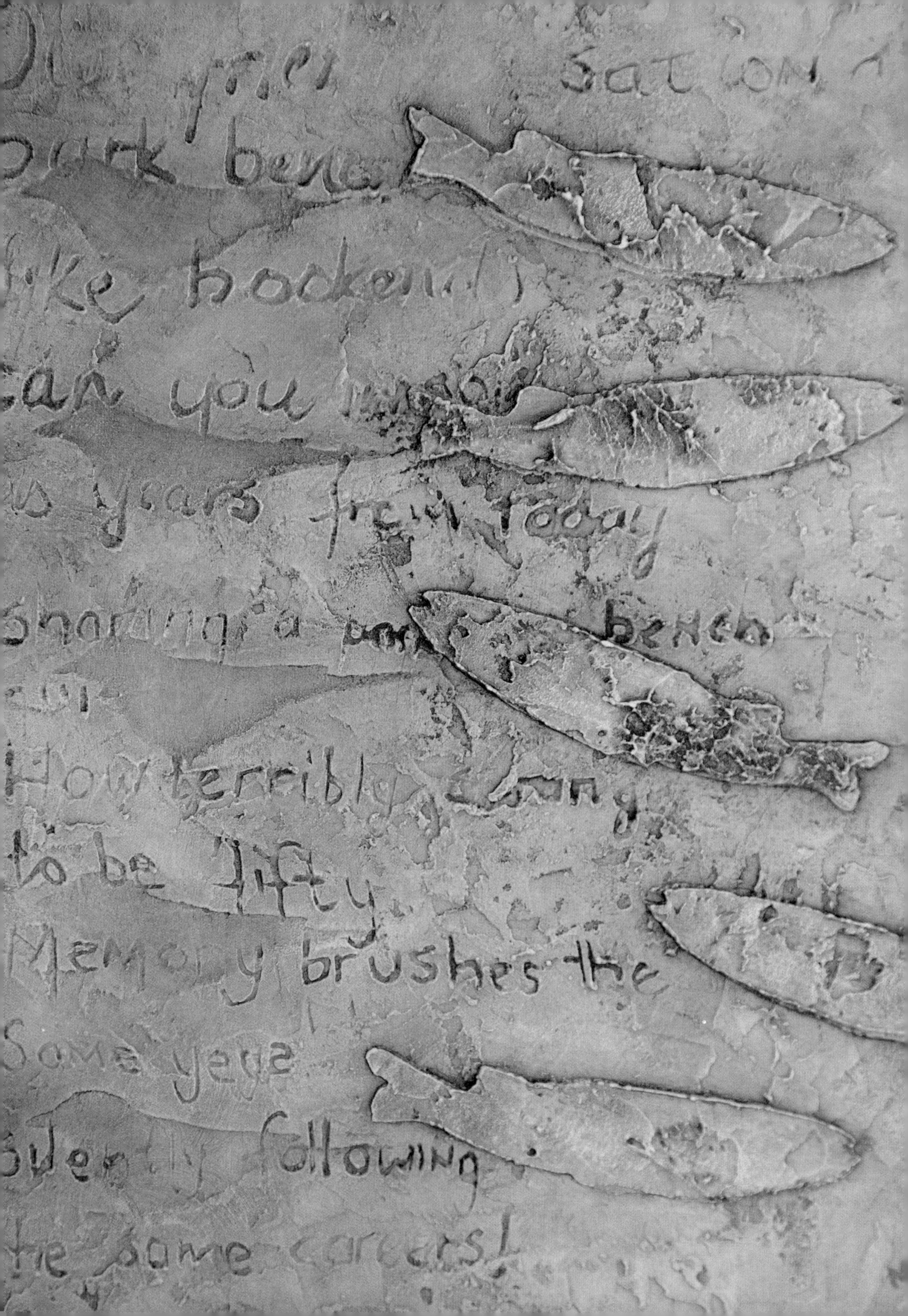

Old friends... Sat on a

park bench...

like bookends

can you imagine

us years from today

sharing a park bench

How terribly strange

to be fifty,

Memory brushes the

same years

silently following

the same careers!

2. Working quite quickly, place the fish stencil in position and scrape crack filler through the fish shape so that the fish is raised from the rest of the card. Repeat for as many fish as you want. Place them at slightly different angles and turn the stencil over so that they 'swim' in different directions – don't forget to wipe the stencil off between applications. Fill in any black still visible through the bird shape with a thin layer of crack filler. While the crack filler is wet, scrape your saying or verse into it with the kebab stick or nail. Write over the birds but avoid the fish.

3. Wait for the crack filler to dry or speed up by drying with a hairdryer. Paint the panel in a patchy way using burnt sienna, viridian, blue and lots of white. Leave to dry and then drybrush the texture with white acrylic to enhance it.

4. Mix a little Payne's grey oil paint with oil medium. This both thins the oil and speeds up drying time. Paint over the entire work with this.

5. Using a soft clean cloth, wipe away the oil, leaving the grey in the cracks. The previously drybrushed white will also stand out.

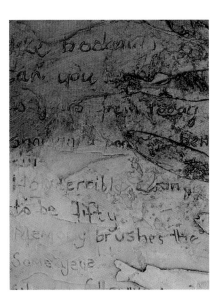
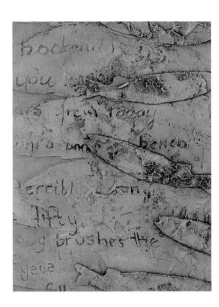

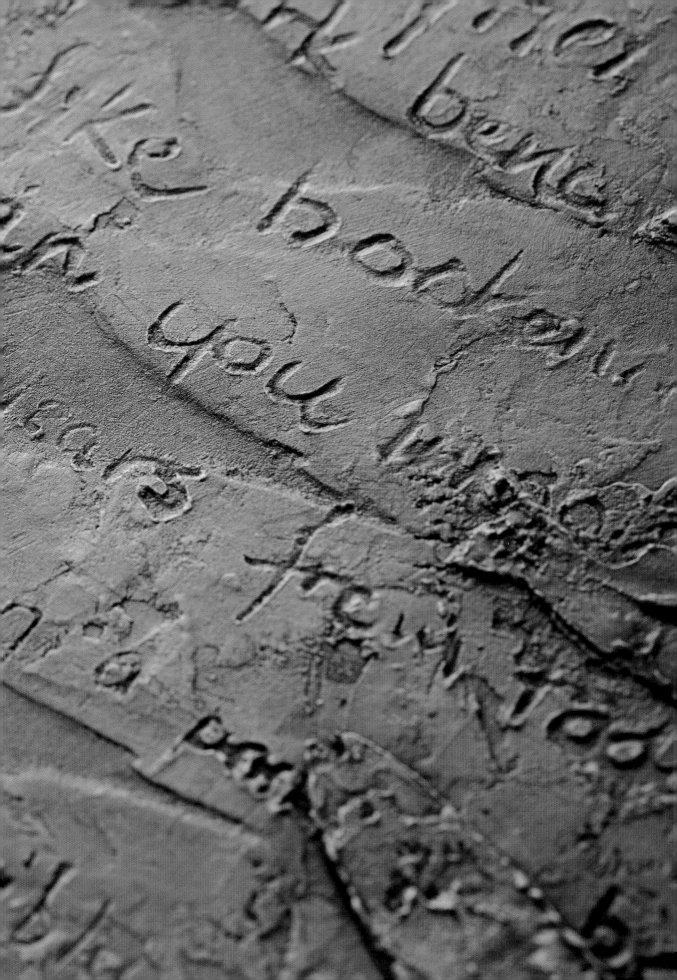

Aloe Ferox

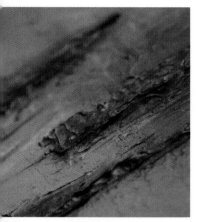

Assimilate single ink-jet print or photo with texture paste, bandages and painting for a softly sculptured feel.

An aloe is a prickly subject and the shape quite hard and spikey. For this reason I decided to treat the image as softly as possible using a photo, lots of texture and a very limited palette, creating a feeling of the hot African sun. I'm always reminded of my late aunt when the aloes are in flower. Hailing from the cold north, it's no wonder she was completely fascinated by them. If you feel you can't draw then this technique is a cinch.

You will need

- Support – I used white mount board
- Enlarged photocopied image in black and white
- Cold glue
- Texture/modelling paste
- Additions – I used tissue paper, sand and crepe bandage
- Spatula, credit-type card or palette knife
- Acrylic paint in Payne's grey, burnt sienna, burnt umber, French ultramarine and white
- Variety of paintbrushes
- Hairdryer – optional

1. Paste the photocopy into position and roll a brayer over it to make sure it is well glued and that the air bubbles are removed. Allow the glue to dry.

2. Using the palette knife or card, plaster the bottom part of the picture with a thick layer of texture paste – as much 'texture' as you like.

3. Push some bandage and tissue paper into the paste to vary the texture. For fun, I pushed a stamp into the tissue paper at the bottom left to leave an impressed image. I also added some fine sand to the texture paste on the bottom right for roughness.

4. Apply a thinner layer of paste to the top area of the picture, over the edges of the photocopy so that they are not so obvious when you paint them later. I added triangles of texture above the main aloe for the flowers. By the time I photographed them, the flowers had all died. Wait for the texture to dry. This may take more than 24 hours, depending on the weather.

5. Paint the bottom of the picture with Payne's grey, drybrushing as you continue up the image. Do make sure that the bandage has been painted dark as this enhances the texture later.

6. Paint the bottom of the picture in a patchy way using burnt sienna, burnt umber and a little white. Add interest by painting rocks just underneath the aloes. These are really just blobs of colour with dark added for shading – a mix of Payne's grey and burnt umber. Add highlights with a mix of white, burnt sienna and burnt umber.

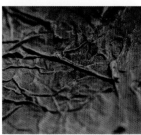

7. Paint in the sky area with a similar, but lighter mix of burnt sienna, Payne's grey and white. Stroke the textured triangles with burnt sienna and voila, aloe flowers. Time to reassess the picture: the aloes need darker shading and some highlights, while the stones are much too even and woolly. They also need more shadow.

8. Use thinned Payne's grey to define the leaf shapes in the aloe and a mix of burnt sienna and white as a highlight. I used the dark mix in the stones and applied the same highlight with a dry brush. I painted in the stems of the aloe flowers and dabbed them off to appear a little vague.

9. Finally, highlight all the textured areas with a very light mix of white and burnt sienna. The lighter texture at the top of the picture must be dry-brushed with Payne's grey to define it a little more.

Amber

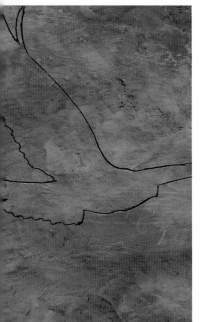

Integrating photos, ink-jet prints and objects by embedding in wax, give a translucence to this encaustic painting and engraving.

Let me introduce you to Amber, who, when these pictures were taken, was just about eight weeks old and had never flown before. She was discovered in a nest when a tree was chopped down. She is now flying free and due to be released soon. We have been home to a number of birds of prey over the last few years on their way to being nurtured, nursed and released. Joshua has taken a great interest in bird rehabilitation, so I am able to get up close and personal and can take photographs to my heart's delight. I wanted to do a simple artwork encapsulating these photos and a couple of feathers without changing or working on the photos themselves. Wax as a medium is perfect for such a project: it can embed items or be layered, engraved and coloured with oil paints.

You will need

- Support – I used the lightest wood I could find: plywood
- Photos and any other things you wish to embed
- Beeswax – clear
- Encaustic coloured wax – I used venetian red, bright blue, light blue, purple and a little yellow
- Hot tray
- Flat metal baking tray to melt clear beeswax
- Muffin baking pan (or other small metal containers)
- Heat gun
- Large flat paintbrush – assigned for wax only.
- Medium soft brush for oil paint
- Metal palette knife
- Sharp tool or nail
- Payne's gray oil paint and artist linseed oil (if needed)
- Soft, clean cloth

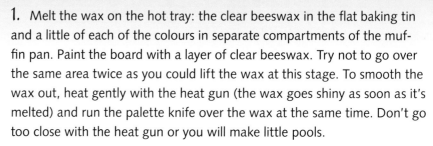

1. Melt the wax on the hot tray: the clear beeswax in the flat baking tin and a little of each of the colours in separate compartments of the muffin pan. Paint the board with a layer of clear beeswax. Try not to go over the same area twice as you could lift the wax at this stage. To smooth the wax out, heat gently with the heat gun (the wax goes shiny as soon as it's melted) and run the palette knife over the wax at the same time. Don't go too close with the heat gun or you will make little pools.

2. Tear the edges of the photos. Slide the first photo into the clear beeswax in the flat baking tin. As quickly as possible, place it in position on the prepared wax board. Fuse the layers of wax by gently heating with the heat gun and using the palette knife to smooth it out. Leave to cool down and set.

3. I used the colours in the photos to guide me as to what colours to mix. I wanted to keep them soft too, so I used a lot of clear beeswax with the blues and the venetian red while the dirty purple was made with purple, a touch of yellow and beeswax. Paint around the photo using your colour mixes, just as you would with any paint. Don't overwork as you could lift the wax at this stage. To fuse the wax, heat and smooth as in step 2. Leave to cool down and set.

4. Slide the second photo into the clear beeswax and again, as quickly as possible, place in position and fuse again by heating and then smoothing with the palette knife. Leave to cool down and set.

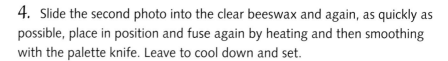

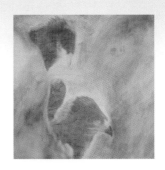

5. Paint around this photo, blending the colours to work in with the first photo. This time paint to the edges of the board, completely covering the wood. When you are happy with the result, heat and fuse as usual. Leave to cool down and set.

6. Cut out the shape of a bird from a photo or drawing and place it in position on the wax surface. Using a sharp tool or nail, gently scrape a groove around the shape and brush away any excess wax.

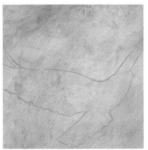

7. Place one feather in position, and paint over with clear beeswax, making sure it is well covered. Repeat for the second feather. Gently heat the wax again with the heatgun and smooth out with the palette knife.

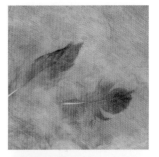

8. When the wax is completely cool, paint with Payne's gray oil paint using a soft brush. If your paint is a bit thick it may be thinned down with a little linseed oil. The oil paint will get into all the nooks and crannies of the slightly uneven wax, enhancing the texture and emphasising the outlines of the bird. Rub off with a soft cloth. Keep folding the cloth to keep the surface clean.

Oil and bubble

Ink-jet prints embedded in wax and coloured with oil paint.

Global warning: global warming! Our life-cycle is threatened from the ever-dwindling fish in polluted waters, to the predators (including us) who consume them. This piece was inspired by a series of photos of drain covers (the bubbles), which struck me while travelling through New Zealand. The proximity of the sea, proliferation of rivers and the fact that many covers are marked with fish symbols, implying that waters feeding through them will empty into the ocean, make an impact that drier, land-bound countries can comfortably ignore. This is a gift for Melinda and Martin who tuned in to my crusading quest for quirky 'cover pics' with great enthusiasm.

You will need

- Black and white ink-jet copies or photocopies of fish (I used a sardine image from a recipe book and enlarged it to several sizes)
- Coloured ink-jet prints of drain covers (I reduced these to several sizes)
- Craft knife and scissors
- Canvas (I used a ready primed A3 sheet from a canvas block)
- Pollutants. I used what I could find in the garage, shed and kitchen – from brake fluid and used engine oil to thinners, used dye and detergents – anything that goes down our drains to the sea – this is 'extreme' mixed media.
- Wax crayons
- Fine point black permanent marker
- Beeswax, empty tin can, candle and stand, old hog-hair brush
- Darning needle or sharp stylus
- Oil paints – burnt umber, burnt sienna and rose madder
- Large soft mop brush
- Artists turpentine
- Soft nylon cloth (old stocking will do)

1. Using the craft knife, cut the fish carefully from the prints so that you have a stencil window space left for each size fish. Set the fish aside and draw rough wax crayon strokes through the stencil windows onto the canvas. I let all my fish swim in one direction – to the left to symbolize those still left. At this point I only drew in three whole and two half-off-the-edge fish shapes in grey, pink and white crayons.

2. The next step was to pour all the pollutants over the canvas in a horizontal direction. I left the mess to soak overnight and scrubbed it well the next morning with more detergents and thinners to remove the excess oily residues. Once the canvas was rinsed and almost dry, I sandwiched it between layers of brown paper and newsprint and ironed it flat and dry. It really did look suitably distressed and polluted at this stage. The crayoned fish were almost completely obliterated by the pollutants – the symbolism was satisfying.

3. I redrew some more fish with crayons and the fine permanent marker to simulate a subtle background of shadowy fish in a shoal.

4. The same colours of crayon with the addition of pink bring life to the black and white fish cut-outs in this step. I set up the candle as a burner beneath the stand holding the tuna tin containing beeswax and lit it. When the wax was melted and very hot, I used the old hog-hair brush to 'glue' the fish shapes into position on the canvas. You can use a hairdryer to help melt the wax. Hold the fish in position until the wax cools and they stick down completely. Layer fish over other fish or the crayon drawings for a shoal effect.

5. At this stage I spent ages cutting out all the tiny copies of the drain covers I had printed – my daughters were not impressed... But once they were 'glued' in position with more melted wax, they revealed their purpose as polluted 'air bubbles' and suddenly made sense in the scheme of the picture.

6. I diluted the oil colours with artists' turpentine and glazed colour over the wax, blending the rose through sienna to umber from the top to the bottom of the picture.

Note: Wax should only be coloured with oil-based paints or wax shoe polish.

 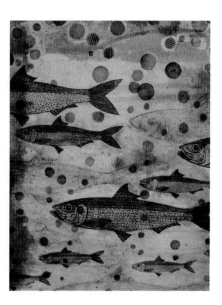 

Safe Harbour

Pouring, plastic wrap texture, drawing and painting with a credit-type card blend vibrancy and texture to this composite painting.

We are all taught to colour inside the lines as children and while there is a certain merit to this, it can be tremendously inhibiting in a painting. What if you were to colour in before there were any lines? By combining different types of paper with two of my favourite techniques in this painting (pouring – or running – and scraping with a credit card), I've created a layered, textured painting with simple shapes. A leisurely Sunday visit to the Hout Bay fishing harbour, not too far from us, provided the opportunity to take a collection of colourful photographs. These were the inspiration for this painting. If you'd like to explore more of this style, mixed-media artist Mike Bernard works in a similar way.

You will need

- Plain paper and a pencil – use your creative journal
- Support – I used a canvas, though a harder support like wood actually works better when gluing paper
- Paper of whatever kind for gluing on the canvas: newsprint, tissue paper, magazine pages, painted paper, etc.
- Glue – cold glue is fine
- Paintbrushes
- Brayer
- Acrylic paint – I used phthalo blue, cerulean blue, deep madder, cadmium red, viridian, white and black (acrylic inks would also work)
- Plastic wrap
- Credit-type card

1. Working from a photograph is acceptable (though many artists would disagree), but it can offer too much information so that the composition becomes cluttered and overworked. Simplify the subject by making a sketch of the most useful information. Sketching in front of the actual scene is always best.

2. Without drawing on the canvas, though having an idea of the composition from the sketch, glue paper in the areas you feel will be most effective. Don't be too pernickety – you don't want to 'colour in' with the paper. Make sure the paper is well glued, paying particular attention to the edges. Roll a brayer over the paper to get rid of any air bubbles. A canvas has a tendency to be a bit 'soft' in the middle. Put a book or other hard surface underneath to bolster it while brayering.

3. Spray the canvas lightly with water. Paint washes in rose, cadmium red, cerulean and phthalo blue with a wide brush. Allow the paint to run, mixing on the canvas. Note that the reds are in the vague area of the boats while the blues are in the sky and sea area. The colours of the pasted papers shine through. Leave to dry or speed up with a hairdryer.

4. Repeat the process, adding viridian this time. Allow to run across the canvas. Before the paint dries, place on a flat surface and cover the sea area with plastic wrap. Allow to dry. You can repeat this step if you feel you don't have enough coverage.

5. Now things get really interesting. Draw in the black outlines with the credit card – I dare you. The lines will be very uneven – all the better. These outlines will give you a sense of placement and composition.

6. Still using a credit card (a clean one), add white in the areas where you will need highlights (lighter areas) on the boats and also in the sea and sky – go over the edge of the paper to soften the result. This is a relatively patchy effect.

7. Colour the sky with cerulean blue, allowing the white to shine through. Paint the mountains to tone in with the paper – in this case viridian and permanent rose – allowing them to mix to make brown here and there. Paint the boats with another light wash, letting the colour run once more. The two outside boats are painted in red and the centre boat in viridian, with the addition of a little yellow. Allow it to run again, adding plastic wrap in the sea area while it dries. The wrinkled plastic enhances the reflection effect.

8. Mix a burnt sienna tone using yellow and red with a spot of blue. Scrape over the white in the bridge area allowing some of the white to show through.

9. Scrape the bridge again with white. As this look is very layered, you can repeat the layering process as often as you feel is necessary – until you have the look you want.

10. Add more black with the edge of a credit card where you feel it necessary – define the masts and ropes and then add white to them to finish your painting.

Memory map

Collage found souvenirs and holiday photos using a map as a stencil onto silk-painted paper.

Kind Kiwi friends extended the warmest of welcomes to me to share time at their 'bach' (holiday home) on beautiful, unspoilt Kawau Island, north-east of Auckland city. The place inspires one from the bluest of green waters to the loftiest redwood trees. Forested slopes of indigenous Kauri pines, Pohutekawa and tree ferns support a variety of fascinating flightless and other fancy birds from bobble-necked Tui to thieving walking Wekas and wild wood pigeons. A memory map of my time with the Louws will hopefully be a welcome gift.

To make your own memory map ...

You will need

- Paper support – I used A2 sheets of textured, handmade mulberry – natural and bleached
- Photocopies of the map of your choice enlarged to whatever size fits the support
- Craft knife and scissors
- Wallpaper and wood glue
- Spray bottle filled with water
- Gel medium
- Varnish and oil paint brushes
- Paint – I used silk (sun) paints and acrylics
- Dishwasher or rock salt crystals
- Memorabilia – I used torn photos, pages from a book about Governor George Grey (of New Zealand and South Africa), prints of images, gift wrapping tissue, skeleton and dried leaves, ferns, sand, tiny shells, feathers
- Oil paint sticks in viridian, azure and titanium white
- Printed poetry or prose – I wrote my memories of my stay in prose form
- Cardboard chip lettering
- Water-based satin varnish

KAWAU
Island

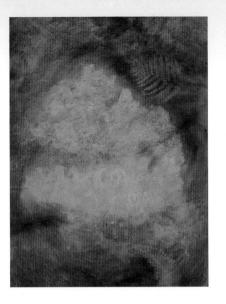 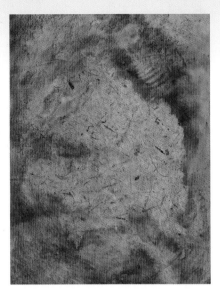 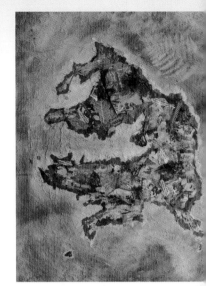

1. Cut out the enlarged island from the map and use the island shaped 'hole' as a stencil to through which to paint thick wallpaper glue onto the sheet of bleached mulberry paper. Remove the stencil, spray the surrounding paper damp and paint washes of diluted silk paints in greens and blues into the area around the gluey island shape. I sprinkled the wet paint with salt crystals and placed a dried fern leaf flat onto the painted surface before laying the paper out in a sunny, windless spot to dry. The salt pulled the paints into points of colour while the fern bleached its image under the sun's influence on the silk paint.

2. Use the solid photocopied island cut out as a template for duplicating the island shape in heavy textured, buff-coloured, mulberry paper. I laid the photocopy onto the paper and brushed water off the edges. This soaked onto the surrounding paper enabling me to tear the dry island shape easily from its wet surround. Stick the dry, textured 'island' down in position on the blue-green, silk-painted paper with wallpaper glue. Any torn pieces or gaps are easily patched with scraps of textured paper and wallpaper glue. Use the photocopy shape to check that the map shape is correct.

3. Tear all pictures, photos, pages and tissue paper into small enough relevant pieces to collage all over the island. Smooth down well with wallpaper glue and add tiny shells, feathers, sand, dried and skeleton leaves in places where there may be gaps. I used the green tissue paper to fill spaces which added to the overall 'greenness' I was aiming for.

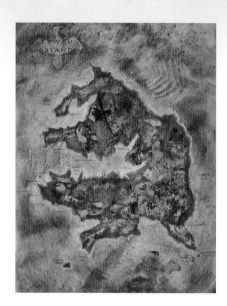

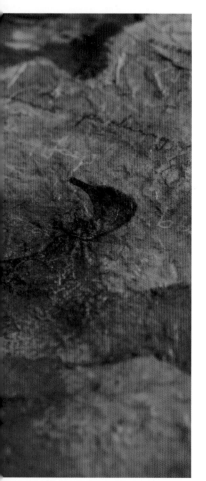

4. Unify the collage by washing the island area (except the 'beach-coloured' edges of mulberry paper) with a dilute mix of green (copper oxide) acrylic paint and water mixed with a little water-based varnish to extend the paint and delay the drying time. You may want to lighten your paint effect here and there so that images in the torn photos are more clearly visible. I tried to keep faces less green than the rest of the images.

5. Add place names using your chosen method. Either write or print directly by hand using gel or ballpoint pens (others will bleed), or transfer printed words from transparencies using your computer, transparency film for ink-jet printers and gel medium. Remember to print wording mirror-imaged or flipped as you will reverse the film when transferring. Paint a little gel medium in the position of the place name; place the printed name, ink-side down, into position and burnish with your fingernail. Lift the film carefully to check that the lettering has transferred evenly. If not, add a little more medium, line up the print and re-burnish firmly using the bowl of a teaspoon.

6. Kawau is a Maori word meaning shag or cormorant, so I cut a paper stencil from an A4 print of a cormorant. The stencil cut out shape is used in two ways. I used it as a block-out or mask around which I lightly rubbed viridian and azure oil paint sticks to reveal a negative or lighter cormorant shape against the 'sea'. The stencil window shape was placed in position at the base of the island and more oil paint stick rubbed through it with the addition of a little titanium white to reveal another cormorant shape in a positive, darker silhouette in reverse.

7. I copied my 'memory' prose directly onto the 'sea' using a random mix of gel pens in copper, gold, white, lime and aquamarine green. Some words cannot be read easily and I deliberately wrote some lines muddled between others. The effect is one of a continuous wave in the style of the writing. Stream of consciousness describes the way our minds work with random recorded thoughts flowing without punctuation. My memories come back to me as a sea of jumbled occurrences, imagery and feelings. Hopefully the writing captures this. It is intensely personal and not intended to be read as much as contribute to the overall feel of the piece.

8. This type of artwork needs to be varnished or sealed to hold all the pieces together to form a cohesive whole as well as preserve the colours and strengthen all the components. I used a few layers of podge, drying well between them. It was at this point that I felt the title Kawau Island needed more emphasis as the original transfer was too small in scale and the font too simple. I found these chip letters at a scrapbooking shop to suit before imbedding them in the podge. A few final coats of water-based satin sealer completed the process. The artwork is now flat and flexible enough to mail in a tube to the Louws.

The gathering

A combination and integration of painted brown paper, Tyvek, Lutradur, interfacing, heated copper, corrugated board, stitching and stamping create this lively gathering.

The past year has seen me part of a number of significant gatherings of people, both in celebration and in mourning. I have used a wide variety of materials to symbolise the many characters and personalities embraced in the same ritual. The limited palette signifies the unity of our purpose of being at the time. If you are unable to source some of the materials, simply substitute for something else that crosses your path.

You will need

- Corrugated board from an old box
- Brown paper painted and crackled and stamped
- Lutradur, Tyvek, appliqué paper, iron-on interfacing or substitute with other materials
- Teflon sheet for ironing if using Tyvek, Lutradur and appliqué paper
- Iron
- Acrylic paint in burnt sienna, red oxide, cadmium red, process cyan, Payne's grey and copper
- Copper paint stick
- Brushes – a variety
- Stamps (optional)
- Copper sheet
- Small gas-filled blowtorch or other source of heat
- Sewing machine (or sew by hand) with needle size 70 and 90/100
- Sewing thread
- Chalk pastels in red and turquoise
- Gel medium
- Red embroidery thread and needle

1. Draw your composition to scale and cut the figures out of scrap paper to make a pattern piece of each one. Don't toss them when you're done – use them in your journal.

2. For the background support, paint 3 large pieces of brown paper in different shades and tones of burnt sienna, red, brown and white. I used layers of paint in different textures to create the effect. The paper was crinkled, drybrushed, scraped and one piece rubbed on a texture plate with a copper paint stick. Iron the paper on the back every now and then to smooth out.

3. Using the pattern pieces, prepare the figures by cutting them out of the various materials:

  a. Create crackled effects by first painting brown paper dark blue and then, when dry, painting with crackle medium and/or cold glue (I made a strip of each). Paint the crackle medium with red when dry, but paint the glue red when it forms a skin and is still slightly white. Each method will produce a somewhat different crackle effect. Stamp a pattern onto the taller figure using copper paint.

  b. Cut out the corrugated figure and then partially cut away a section of a figure, and tear to reveal the corrugations. Paint this, and the heavily textured handmade paper figures, with Payne's grey. Drybrush with red, to varying degrees. The corrugated box figure should be drybrushed again with copper paint.

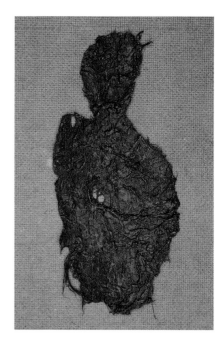

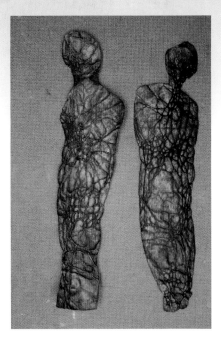

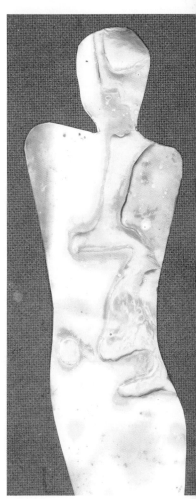

c. Paint the appliqué paper figure with red and Payne's grey. The paint separates and, when dry, creates a lovely textured effect. Similarly, paint the iron-on interfacing. The effect is much smoother so I added a texture by rubbing with the copper paint stick over a texture plate, in the same way as I did with the brown paper.

d. Tyvek shrivels when heated creating a stunning textured effect. The figures should be cut larger than the pattern. It can be heated using an iron (a Teflon sheet must be used), or with a heat gun. It can be painted before or after heating. I used an iron for these two figures, both of which were painted before heating. The Teflon, placed between the iron and the Tyvek, should be touched lightly with the iron, or the Tyvek will shrivel more than you want. The bubble effect will depend on which side down you place the painted sheet.

e. Lutradur also reacts when heated, creating a webbed effect. It shrinks too, and should be cut larger to begin with. You can paint it before or after heating, though thicker paint may react as a resist.

f. Heat copper sheet with a small gas-filled blowtorch to create a colourful variegated effect. A candle, stove or other heat source may be used for different effects. Cut out or use a small diamond punch for the shapes to be added later. You could work into the copper adding a pattern, as you would with pewter, though I chose not to.

4. Phew, now that you've introduced yourself to all your figures, let's start on the background. Sew the three layers of painted brown paper together. I sewed the 'sandwich' together in two areas using a straight stitch, the first about one third in and the second about a sixth from the right. The piece in the middle was the uppermost, while the piece visible on the left was at the bottom. The top strip was torn roughly along the outside of each 'seam' to reveal the paper below. This was torn in turn on the left to reveal the bottom paper. We now have three different papers showing.

5. For added texture, stamp lightly at the top right and bottom left, using process cyan and a square stamp.

6. Draw the central figure in the centre panel and sew around the shape. Tear the top layer of paper away on the inside of the sewing to reveal the paper below.

7. Glue the group of figures in front of this in place and sew around each one. Repeat again for the following group until all but the copper and corrugated board figures are in place.

8. The edges of the figures appear quite 'hard', so, to integrate them into the background, I used chalk pastels. Work with one colour at a time. I started with turquoise. Scribble around the more turquoise figures – the colour appears too bright but is dulled in the next step.

9. Paint on a little gel medium, with a soft brush. Don't overwork, and clean the brush often (wipe off in your journal). The gel blurs and fixes the pastel at the same time. Leave to dry or speed up with a hairdryer.

10. Repeat the process using a deeper red or red oxide chalk pastel, this time around the red figures.

11. Stitch the copper figure in place using a thick needle (90/100). Add three red crosses to the right side, using embroidery thread.

12. Hand stitch the corrugated board in place with the red embroidery thread.

13. Stitch the small copper diamonds in place using ordinary red sewing thread.

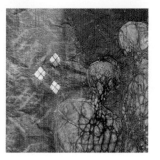

Be still

Your innermost sense of self, of who you are, is inseparable from stillness. This is the I Am that is deeper than name and form.

Eckhart Tolle

Combed and stamped paste paper, cut, torn and collaged with shellac and pigment powders.

It's quite an art getting to befriend your 'self'. I find when I am alone and busy with right-brained activities my swirling, jumbled thoughts begin to still and I get into a calm zone. So many people who come to painting lessons find the need to balance the busyness of day-to-day left-brain activity with right-brained intuitive exploration and simply letting go. I find great value in these time-out sessions with my right brain, exploring and befriending my self. Slowly I learn to be gentler with my self, less focused on right and wrong and more accepting of my being – warts and all.

This particular project was a good way to use up those odd bits created from messing and playing with leftover paints, paste and scrap paper – and the results didn't have to match up to the 'perfect' picture I'd started out with in my head. I had to let that go as well – and learn to accept this result in its imperfection. Try your own version of letting go from your head and allowing art to start from your heart.

You will need

- Newspaper
- Spray paint – I used gold
- Card
- Paste – see glossary for recipe
- Rubber combs or tile adhesive applicators
- Pigment powder – I used gold
- Acrylic colours of your choice
- Stamps – I used the spiral and the Adinkra fern as they have much meaning for me
- Any objects that will leave impressions – I used a grid of tile spacers
- Copy paper with printed inspirational word(s)
- Crackle glaze – I used the two part small crack base and top coat
- Shellac
- Podge

ARTFUL WAYS WITH MIXED MEDIA

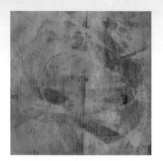

1. I wanted to explore the notion of 'being still' and as we were taught 'silence is golden' by the dear Irish nuns who tried to control our chatter at school, I thought gold would be a good colour on which to base this exploration. Earlier I had spray-painted something for another project with gold lacquer spray and used newspaper as a protective mask. The shiny paint coloured the newspaper in varying shades of gold with some text peeping through, leaving me with a perfect first layer.

2. I needed something dark as a contrast or foil for the gold, so I crumpled some paper and brushed it with black PVA that had a greenish base. I tried to make this piece look mysterious – like a still, misty night sky.

3. Next I scraped some uncoloured paste onto sheets of dark card and left it to dry partially. These pieces were dusted with pigment powder and left to dry completely before brushing off the excess powder with a soft brush.

4. I then mixed acrylic colours into the remaining paste and covered several pieces of light card with rich hues in various combinations: combing, scraping, impressing and stamping into the wet goo until I had enough. These spoke to me of all the busyness I indulge in most of the time. They took two days to dry leather-hard, teaching me that patience is also part of 'being still'. I chose one piece I liked for my collage.

ARTFUL WAYS WITH MIXED MEDIA

5. All the time I was playing with paints and paste the well-known verse 10 from Psalm 46 was running though my left-brain: "Be still and know that I am God". Some further consideration of this verse took me from "Be still and know that I am" to "Be still and know" to simply "Be still" and "Be". I printed this out onto copy paper and sealed it with shellac.

6. Now that I had the words as well as the colours and textures, I played around with cutting, tearing and arranging. I tore a scrap of the spray-painted newspaper into a spiral, then took it a step further and tore an edge off the spiral all the way until it unwound into a negative and positive split. This felt right and I went ahead bravely and stuck it all together using a varnish brush and podge – no longer caring if it was 'right' or good enough or too weird. It is what it is and it will continue to remind me that I am who I am.

7. There's a further lesson in knowing when enough is enough. I tried to get clever by adding stitching. This didn't work and disappointed and frustrated my 'stillness' of being. I brushed over some pigment and varnish burying the sewing with more golden simplicity.

Notes: Aya, the fern, is the Adinkra symbol of endurance and resourcefulness. The spiral is a universal symbol for evolving into being, the journey of life and the cyclical nature of the feminine being. The grid is a symbol of knowing boundaries as well as the ability to network and communicate.

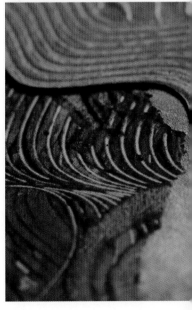

Beach break

Collage photographs, paste-papers, advertisements and lettering with fake pewter, sand and gold embossing.

I miss my early beach walks as I drive my daughter to work. Sarie and Lindsay take my dog with them instead, so this card expresses my gratitude (and longing). Sarie maintains daily walking and coffee on the beach is the best health cure.

I found some ancient *Huisgenoot* magazines (dated from 1923) in the roof of a student house and wanted to use the crumbling, sand-coloured paper and quaint advertisements. I printed a picture of Sarie with her coffee cup in sepia tones on my ink-jet printer and sealed it with clear lacquer spray so that water-based glue wouldn't make it bleed. Coffee beans and grounds, the aluminium seal of a coffee can, sea-sand, turquoise sea-glass, a flattened bottle cap from the beach car park and a chocolate wrapper add quirky embellishments. Sea colours and textures torn from decorated papers add a further dimension. Gold embossing powder accents the coffee aroma swirls. A faint scent of coffee and the grainy texture of sea sand create atmosphere. To make a similar collage ...

You will need

- Advertisements and articles from old magazines – charity shops may throw out torn vintage magazines.
- Personal photographs printed in sepia tones
- Wallpaper glue
- Wood glue
- Paintbrushes
- Aluminium coffee tin seals
- Knitting needle or dry ballpoint pen
- Piece of felt
- Burnt umber oil paint
- Pieces of torn paper – I used painted, paste, brown, bitumen and tissue paper
- Embellishments: I used sea glass, chocolate wrapper, coffee bean, coffee grounds, metal bottle cap, flat glass blob, sea sand, embossing powder
- Purple acrylic paint

1. I tore out some old coffee advertisements as well as some apt headlines. I composed them, together with the picture of Sarie, and scraps of torn paste papers, as the 'bones' of my picture.

2. Using a pewter moulding tool (a knitting needle) I copied the simple line-drawn coffee cup from the main advertisement, enlarging and indenting it into the textured aluminium coffee seal. I reversed the seal to rub the cup relief gently, flattening the texture overall, before turning it over again. A finger dab of burnt umber oil paint rubbed into the indentations added depth and an antique look. When dry, I cut it from the seal.

3. I glued the glass blob to the bottle top with wood glue for a quirky sun; the chocolate wrapper made a halo enhancing 'Koffie'; the cup covered the gap under the coffee pot; the sea glass marked the 'water line'.

4. I mounted the collage on a darker background to frame it and enhance the colouring. I tore and separated the bitumen paper sandwich. The pieces toned perfectly as a backdrop. The brown paper backing to the bitumen stuck easily to card with wallpaper glue.

5. The collage stuck fast to the bitumen surface with wood glue. I added more paste paper, lettering and torn bits of painted and tissue paper to fill further gaps with more wood glue. This had to dry thoroughly before the next step.

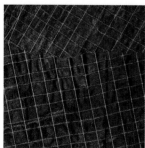

6. I squeezed lines of wood glue between gaps and painted glue around some raised bits before shaking sea sand over the whole picture and leaving it to dry.

7. Wood glue, painted into the coffee cup relief and sprinkled with coffee grounds, filled it to the brim with real coffee. The coffee bean, stuck with more wood glue, enhanced the 'Koffie' halo. This had to dry before any excess grounds could be shaken off.

8. Diluted purple acrylic added more colour and pushed the centre of the picture back, thus seating the photo of Sarie into the background.

9. Brushing over the purple with wallpaper glue lightened and blended it. This had to dry before I could paint the aroma swirls with more wallpaper glue. These were covered with gold embossing powder and the excess gently tapped off. A heat gun melted the powder swirls to a shiny focus above the cups.

Journals and books

Journals

The word journal comes from the French, meaning *a daily recording of something, traditionally in written form*. Journals and ledgers are used in bookkeeping, but the term means something much more personal and exploratory in art. Art journals are not a 'Dear Diary', nor are they simply a sketchbook, nor just a recording of ideas. Put the whole lot together and you're probably nearer to what they are. They provide a place, private or not, to record ideas, images and thoughts in a way that facilitates the creative process – a connection between the written and the visual.

Supports can vary from bought and bound journals, bits of paper worked on and eventually bound large envelopes, flyers, old books, diaries and even bookkeeping journals. Paint and paste over lines and text as this will merely add texture to your experiments. We both have a tendency to scribble on scrap paper. Sometimes we collect and bind these pages into swatch books, ripe for interesting additions or ready to be given as gifts to arty friends.

While journals help one organize ideas, inspiration and experiments, they are by nature, fairly haphazard. Your book may include finished work; it could just include sketches and notes for other projects – a notebook for creative brainstorming. It provides an opportunity to build up a personal image library and keep track of artistic development, written and visual responses, e.g. a gratitude journal will record personal images that generate a sense of appreciation, while a journal of insects may focus on the minutiae of entomological life. Sometimes art journaling can be a natural progression from scrapbooking as the lines between them become blurred.

Discard boring book jackets and cover or create your own to suit that personal collection. This assortment of covers spans handmade books as well as altered book covers.

ARTFUL WAYS WITH MIXED MEDIA

The scroll book begged to be rolled up into a crusty log of striated bark. This was achieved with puff paint brushed onto battered corrugated cardboard and then drybrushed for effect. The finishing touch was a tie of crocheted fine copper wire embellished with tiny cones and a feather. All it needs now is the filling – a cute little story to unroll about a worm boring from the centre of the book and becoming a butterfly in the process.

Torn sheets of handmade and decorated paper make up the swatch book. The cover was fashioned from a piece of corrugated cardboard ripped from a box flap and covered with heavily embossed, handmade paper. The swatch pages and covers are held together with screw posts – commonly used for wallpaper books and album covers. The front cover is decorated with inchies torn from matching papers. Scribbled lines of poetry fill odd pages as the mood moves the creative spirit to write.

Turning over a new leaf is the decoupaged title of the index book. The pile of leaves, some real, one wooden, echo the title as well as the pages. These were glued in position with wood glue on a background of painted torn paper. Gold gel pen defines the vein lines and a few glued seeds add interest. The lettering was found in a magazine and altered with pens to suit the aged look. This altered antique book cover serves as a reminder to record borrowings and lendings of precious items.

Peeping out from the large journal, is a handmade album of beach memories for a dear friend in celebration of a special birthday. The hessian wrapped cover holds torn silk pages, stiffened with watered-down wood glue. These are bound together with hessian twine, tied in a bow on the spine. The front cover is scattered with coarse sea sand, crushed shells and a glued seagull feather. The result is a low-key, peaceful folio of photos to browse in contemplative moments.

This leather bound tome is a journal in every sense of the word! Originally a hand-written record of insurance policies, it was rescued from a rubbish heap to be reworked and altered as a mixed media journal. The charcoal card, covering most of the front, is bleached in a linear pattern with a dipping pen and defined with a gel pen. Black webbing spray adds texture. The torn gap is illuminated with the addition of a ragged edged bird shape, echoed in a contrasting shade and emphasised with coloured net and shrivelled Tyvek. Machine stitched lines of metallic and cotton thread sandwich the whole piece together. The gelled end threads add a linear detail down each side. The shabby leather spine, left untouched, keeps its original secrets!

A quirky composite figure comprising six separate photo sections is the focal point of these warm pages, emphasizing a 'point of view/viewpoint' theme. This is flanked by echoing images, pasted and transferred into position with gesso integrating them with the background. A magazine image was added, brushed with matt medium to reduce its glossy surface. Repeated eye images printed on tissue paper link with the eye of Horus stamp. Orange words magically appear on black card by writing with a pen dipped in bleach. Yellow, orange and red warm the picture into life while fine blue texture was 'printed' with scrunched plastic wrap. Wax lines emphasise the angles of the composite figure. Pen outlines emphasize the stance and adorn the eyes with words. Printed and drawn feathers soften the black, adding a touch of mystery.

Bland pages of lines and writing burst into beauty with multilayered techniques. Each method used may be simple in itself, yet worked over progressively, produces a rich texture and transparent depth of colour and meaning. Inspired by these three strong women in my life, a heart motif serviette was decoupaged and coloured with a wash of blue and lime acrylic. Strips of decorated paper and their photos constitute the next layer, covered with a further wash, including orange. The pot was painted in thicker acrylic paint. Bright orange, pink and red florettes were cut from tissue paper, as were the green geranium leaves. Transparent glue allows the tissue layers to blend into a bright floral harmony. Letter and scroll stencils coloured in deeper acrylic tones fill the gaps uniting the elements. Chalk pastels, blended with gel medium add depth to the leaves and flowers, while charcoal lines define detail.

Artists' books

Usually journals are a more haphazard collection and working of ideas while artists' books are developed specifically around a theme – being once-off or very limited editions.

Artists' books can be constructed in many ways including scrolls, concertina folds, a collection of loose sheets in a dedicated box as well as the more obvious bound pages. The covers and pages may also be unique shapes, joined together in a myriad ways, from hand stitched binding to metal links and ribbons.

These unique books are works of art in themselves; different themes will result in as many approaches as there are artists with ideas to integrate image, text and form.

Altered books

Altered books change existing books into works of art. This can be anything from painting over text to sculpting shapes from books. As a fun form of recycling, these quirky books can be shaped to hold ephemera or three-dimensional objects in pockets or niches cut into covers and pages. So don't chuck out your old telephone directories or battered childrens' board books – recycle them into art!

Nature's graffiti

Use watercolour paper, masking fluid, watercolours,
ink and watercolour pencils with the addition of
transfer techniques to make an artist's book.

Artists' books usually have a theme and can be intensely personal or purely
decorative. This is a bit of both. The photo that was used as the main image
for this book was taken at the side of the road on the way to Heathrow
Airport in rather cold weather. I made Michael stop the car while I clicked
away (mutter, mutter ...). I am always amazed at how resilient weeds are –
and how their shapes are often more interesting than those of cultivated
plants and flowers. As Janice Maeditere put it: weeds are nature's graffiti.
I have incorporated sayings written down by my mother in the year before
she died – not a steady hand but meaningful to her, and a lesson to us on
how to keep on going against the odds.

There are quite a number of techniques covered in this project, as well as
five transfer methods. You may not want to use all of them, so you will
find the instructions for the individual transfer techniques in 'Methods' (see
page 122).

You will need

- Watercolour sheet or handmade paper cut or torn into strips and folded
  into a concertina shape – I used two strips joined together eventually
- Watercolours in sap green, cadmium yellow, cadmium red, rose madder,
  Prussian blue
- Masking fluid and old, fine paintbrush
- Acetone
- Spoon
- Watercolour brushes
- Materials for whatever transfer techniques you wish to do (See methods)
- Acrylic ink in black, white and the primaries
- Dipping pen
- Watercolour pencils
- Narrow cotton fabric strip and glue to join your strips of paper

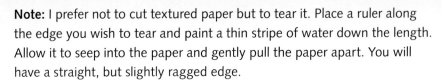

Note: I prefer not to cut textured paper but to tear it. Place a ruler along the edge you wish to tear and paint a thin stripe of water down the length. Allow it to seep into the paper and gently pull the paper apart. You will have a straight, but slightly ragged edge.

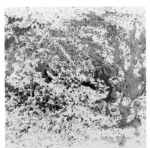

1. Draw your weeds in soft pencil and paint over the lines with masking fluid using a very fine brush. For the finest lines you could even use a skewer. You will need to clean your brush often in acetone as the brush gums up.

2. Splatter yellow and green watercolour paint on the first section of paper quite sparingly, becoming more dense on the second section. Add red, rose and blue.

3. Work the paint in section two together with a brush. While still wet, draw in more weeds with the back of a brush. The paint will pool in these indented lines which will appear darker.

4. Continue adding colour until the one half of the book is covered. I changed subtly from the yellow, orange and red to purple, pink and blue. When dry, paint more weeds in masking fluid and colour the paper in that area again, making it slightly darker. Allow to dry.

ARTFUL WAYS WITH MIXED MEDIA

5. Repeat the same process with the other half of the book, this time shifting from red and yellow spatters to greens and blues. Spatter the end of the book too, so that the spatters are more or less the same as the beginning of the first concertina piece you painted. When both concertina pieces are dry, remove the masking fluid by rubbing gently with your finger. White and coloured weeds will be revealed.

6. At this point I added a number of transfers. Some transfers are more successful than others. Experiment first to see what works for you. If you are unsuccessful on your actual work, you can always use pen and ink to add detail, draw, etc., to get you out of trouble:

a. Tape transfers of lettering: I reversed the printing before making a copy.

b. Solvent transfer with a photocopy and thinners.

c. Gel transfer with a transparency (lifted off). Print the image made on the rough side of the transparency.

d. Gel transfer with a transparency left on and matt medium painted over for further work.

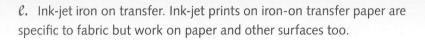

e. Ink-jet iron on transfer. Ink-jet prints on iron-on transfer paper are specific to fabric but work on paper and other surfaces too.

f. A print of a dragonfly was also added: this is not strictly speaking a transfer, but very pleasing, none the less. Tape a piece of tissue paper to normal copy paper and print your image. Cut out and glue into position.

7. Add watercolour pencil drawing onto and over the edges of the transfers to integrate the colours with those you have used. Blend by wetting them slightly with a paintbrush and water. You can also work into the tissue paper transfer with colour.

8. Add more pen and ink drawing and detail in black, white and other colours where you think it necessary.

9. Finer details can be added by pasting tissue paper shapes, stitching and whatever else you can think of – anything goes.

Art cards

As a general term, art cards encompass many types of cards – the list grows all the time.

Each has its own criteria in terms of size and there are various 'rules' and guidelines for each type. The most familiar are:

- **Inchies:** One inch square artwork. (2,54 x 2,54 cm)
- **Rinchies:** One inch (2,54 cm) round artwork. Fit into flattened bottle caps.
- **Twinchies:** Two inch (5,08 cm) square artwork – like an inchie but twice as big.
- **Thrinchies:** Three inch (7,62 cm) square artwork – same concept as inchies and twinchies.
- **Moos:** Made and traded in same way as ATCs. Originally business type card 2,8 x 7 cm (1⅛ x 2¾ in).
- **ATCs** (artists' trading cards): Strictly 9 x 6,35 cm (3½ x 2½ in). Only traded or swapped. Back of cards should have name and contact information. Cards should be numbered. Originated by M. Stirnemann in Zurich, 1997, as a collaborative art project.
- **ACEOs** (art cards, editions and originals): Same as ATCs but for sale.
- **Rolos:** Altered rolodex cards, usually 7,62 x 12,7 cm (3 x 5 in)

So, what do you do with these weird, bitty little things? Displayed as collections around a theme, they can be framed as one artwork, glued onto cards, into bottle caps and used as pendants for unusual jewellery or unique artist's business cards. They're a great way to recycle rejected artworks and birthday or business cards. The exchange of ATCs has become a worldwide networking phenomenon among artists.

These cards should be developed as miniature artworks, rather than just an assemblage of media stamped together with glitter and glue. We've made our own generic cards using variations of our logo to create quirky little pieces in different media from magazine pictures, scraps of paper, paint, gel pens, and embellishments like stars and bugs. The tongues and tails of chameleons and aardvark invited the use of spiral stamps and swirls to complement them.

Faceblock

Our collection of thrinchies showcases faces and profiles using mixed media methods from this book. With copyright issues in mind, we thought we'd be clever and call our fascinating crowd "faceblock". After all, we present our collections on different levels of wooden blocks, adding dimension to the work. This was also an artful opportunity to show off many applications of mixed media. We invite you to get up close and personal with many of our creative characters in the section on methods. You will find tantalizing tips to inspire you to create your own "faceblock" friends. What fun working with a group of "real" friends for special events, each producing one face-block for starters – but that's not where you'll stop!

Our friends all began their lives on 3 inch (7,5 mm) square blocks of 3 mm thick MDF board which we had cut at our local hardware store. Another option is to buy blank coasters from a decoupage supplier. Some blocks were worked on directly while various papers and photos were added to others depending on the technique and media used. We decided to work randomly as we completed projects through the book. Thrinchies are perfect canvases on which to expand ideas and experiment with impunity. It is also a useful way of using up excess mediums towards a collective result. Ours is a motley crew of colour, texture and style – some elegant and some quite scary, a real slice of society. A theme of limited media or method could produce a more homogenous result, for example stencilled black and white faces, with varying details added in pen and ink, would give an overall more focused, graphic effect to change the message on your wall. Suit your faces to their spaces for the ultimate home page status!

Methods

Appliqué paper (fusible web) painting

Painted fusible web distributes a fine irregular mesh of paint texture over the surface to which it is bonded.

Brayering

Spreading ink and paint in a thin even layer with a rubber roller. Also eradicating air bubbles by rolling firmly over glued paper on support.

Chalk pastel blending

Draw and blend softly. Integrate edges. Wet for bold effect.

Combing

Using toothed scrapers to create fine parallel patterns into different viscous mediums, e.g. paste.

Copper heating

Heating copper with a small blowtorch or other heat source creates a range of colour alterations as in fire polishing.

Clouding

Blending of colour while paint is still wet. A very soft hake brush made for this purpose works well. Some areas left lighter create a clouded effect.

Crackling

A two-part process resulting in the top coat or skin drying at a different rate to the base coat, thus pulling the top coat into a pattern of cracks.

Credit-card drawing

Using the sharp edge of a flat plastic card or board, dipped in paint to draw uneven, possibly broken, lines.

Credit-card painting

Using the flat edge of a credit-type card to paste and scrape paint or other media onto the painting surface.

Decoupaging

Cut or tear image from paper and glue to a support with podge, wallpaper glue or wood glue. Seal with varnish to embed finished image in new surface.

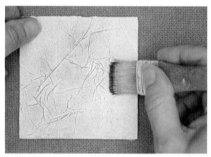

Drybrushing

A light 'scratchy textured' paint effect achieved by flicking a stiff brush with very little paint over a dry surface, building intensity of colour.

Edging

Adding colour or texture specifically around the rim of a painted piece thus adding a finishing and disguising sharp contrasts, e.g. using liquid chalk or metallic markers.

Embossing

Moulding a surface with rounded tools to create relief effects – adding matter, texture or lines to a surface with glue, embossing tools or heat (heat gun).

Engraving

Impress designs or grooves by cutting, carving or etching a surface using tools or chemicals for grooved lines and designs.

Encaustic painting

Painting with encaustic wax using a small dedicated iron, bristle brush or metal palette knife to fuse colours and embed mixed media.

Finger painting

Making marks or applying paint with a finger, fingers or hand.

Foiling

Applying thin film backed material (usually metallic) to glued surface with pressure before peeling backing away.

Gel transfer from paper

Paint copy with gel, place face down onto support. Dry thoroughly, spray back with water and gently rub paper layer off. **Note:** Image transferred in reverse.

Glazing

Thinned colours painted in washes usually diluted with water and specific retarders, but varnishes are also glazes. Can be applied over previously painted areas to modify colour or texture. Also a medium used to facilitate paint effects.

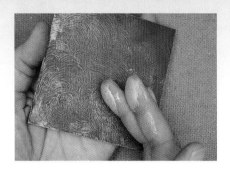

Highlighting

Texture may be highlighted (lightened) by rubbing softly with pigment powder, paint sticks or a drybrush method.

Impressing with a stamp

Impressing a stamp into a thick textural medium to reveal a relief design.

Iron on transfer

Cut ink-jet print to size, place face down in position and iron onto surface.

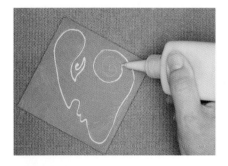

Lining

Paint or other viscous medium applied in lines to surface through the nozzle of a liner bottle.

Lutradur heating

Heat painted or unpainted Lutradur with a heat gun or iron (through a non-stick sheet) to shrivel and alter for textural effects.

Masking

Applying latex-based block-out medium to mask areas from paint. Easily rubbed off surface when dry.

Metal leafing

Applied over tacky glue or size and excess brushed away to reveal metallic finish.

Monoprinting

Transfer a wet painted image from a non-absorbent surface to chosen support.

Negative monoprinting

Transferring a line image from a wet painted sheet to another surface using a pencil or stylus.

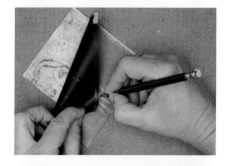

Negative stencilling

Using a solid shape to form a block-out or mask around which to add paint or texture.

Packing tape transfer

Burnish packing tape firmly onto photocopied image or magazine picture. Soak in water, rub off paper and stick image in position. To remove shine, paint with matt medium.

Pen and ink

Dipping pen (with various detachable metal nibs) used with ink to create varying lines and texture.

Plastic wrap texturing

Draping soft plastic over wet paint and allowing it to dry partially or fully revealing wrinkled texture.

Puff painting

Stamp, paint or apply with a liner bottle. Heat with a hairdryer to puff irregularly. Raise to a velvet finish by ironing through a non-stick sheet. Can be painted or drybrushed (to enhance the texture).

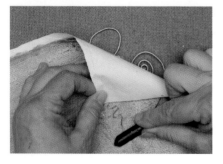

Rubbing

Place paper over raised item or textured plate or surface and rub with contrasting medium so that image or texture is revealed on the paper.

Running

Run water down wet paint allowing it to drip and dribble, creating a watery effect. Pour paint down a support for a similar effect.

Salt texturing

Sprinkle salt onto wet paint to draw it in, leaving a mottled texture.

Sgraffito

Scrape or scratch into wet paint with an implement – silicone shapers, back of brush, erasers, etc.

Shading

Add shadows by blending colour onto edges and contours of flat images to create the illusion of dimension.

Silk (sun) painting

Painting with dedicated paints (see meanings) onto silk or watercolour paper. Use with block-outs to reveal sun exposed images.

Solvent transfer

Transfer photocopied image by rubbing face down with solvent (lacquer thinners or acetone) and burnish with a smooth implement for a pale result. Note that the image is transferred in reverse.

Spattering

Flick, sprinkle, splash or scatter fluid spots with a wet or paint-loaded toothbrush or hard bristle brush.

Stamping

Apply medium onto a stamp with a pad, brush or sponge, roller or brayer. Press stamp onto support to leave image.

Stencilling

Apply medium through stencil window with applicator, e.g. with a stencil brush or sponge for paint, and credit card or palette knife for thicker mediums.

Transparency transfer

Print transparency in reverse on ink-jet printer on photo quality printing option. Place face down onto surface prepared with gel medium. Rub firmly and peel off transparency. As another option, leave transparency in place and coat with matt medium.

Tyvek

Heat painted or unpainted Tyvek with a heat gun or iron (through a non-stick sheet) to shrivel and alter for bubbly textural effects. Bubbles will appear concave or convex, depending on side facing heat source.

Watercolour pencil

Draw, shade and blend with pencils. Wash over with water to dissolve and blend colours further for a watercolour effect.

Wax embedding

Paint melted wax over images or items, sealing them to your chosen support.

Wire bending

Use hands or pliers to bend wire into patterns or shapes.

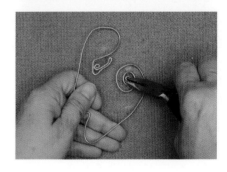

Meanings

Acetone (nail polish remover)

Solvent for epoxies, polyester, polystyrene, fibreglass resins, vinyl, lacquers and adhesives; dissolves grease, oil, and wax.

Acrylic paint

Polyvinyl acetate/acrylic consists of water-based glue with pigment and chalk, drying to a flexible plastic (water-resistant) finish. Acrylics range from the rich clear colours of artists' quality to the bright opaque craft paints and more 'chalky' house paint.

Acrylic palette

Special palette to keep acrylics moist for longer. Homemade version: place a wad of newspaper at the bottom of a plastic container with a tight-fitting lid. Wet newspaper – pour off any excess water. Cover newspaper with baking paper. Squeeze on paint, spray lightly and close lid securely.

Adinkra symbols

West African symbols from Ghana called Adinkra

Alcohol inks

Permanent, acid-free, fast-drying inks. Transparent. Used on non-porous surfaces. Make your own by mixing dye powder with alcohol.

Beeswax

Natural wax from bees. Melts at 62 to 64 °C (144 to 147 °F). Used as an adhesive and covering medium in mixed media and encaustic art.

Bitumen paper

Two craft papers laminated with bitumen for use as water-resistant wrapper. Various weights available in plain or reinforced with glass or metal fibre.

Brayer (rubber roller)

Small, hard hand roller used to spread ink, paint and glue thinly or press decoupage paper evenly onto smooth surfaces.

Calligraphy

The art of beautiful writing.

Canvas

Strong, woven, natural fabric either glued or stretched onto frames or supports. Handmade varieties range in differing weights, surface texture and custom-made sizes. Commercial canvases are ready primed and come in standard sizes. All should have chamfered frames (angled inside edges) to prevent the shadow of the frame showing through the finished painting.

Card stock

Thicker than copy paper and more flexible than paper board. Used for business cards, scrapbooking projects.

Charcoal

Charred black willow twigs rated for thickness of line drawing. Available in less messy pencil form.

Chalk

Available in various forms: chalk sticks (blackboard and pavement chalk), chalk pastels, liquid 'chalk' pads for similar effect.

Crack filler

Smooth paste, bought ready-mixed or in powder form which is mixed with water. Dries to a smooth finish and does not shrink. Not suitable for flexible surfaces, e.g. canvases – rather use flexible or solvent-based foam varieties.

Crackle

Antique varnish or paint finish of fine or large cracks depending on the crackle medium used and how it is applied. Cracks enhanced by rubbing with tinted oil-based glazes. Seal with polyurethane varnish.

Crackle glaze

Crackle glaze (applied between a base and a topcoat) causes the topcoat to crack as it dries, revealing the basecoat through the cracks. There are many types of crackle glaze available including a spray version, but wood glue works as a substitute. Size, number and direction of cracks will depend on the thickness and direction of application of the glaze and topcoat.

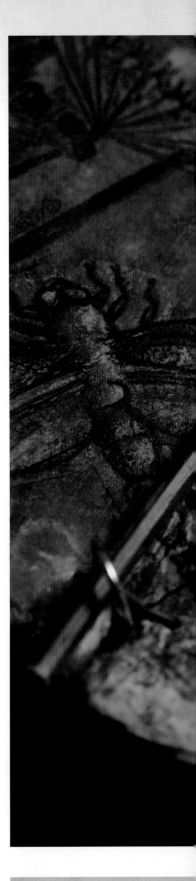

Cold/white/wood glue

White PVA multipurpose glue that dries clear. It bonds porous materials such as wood, cardboard, paper and natural fibres. Can be thinned with water. Also used for strength when mixing powder textures like finishing plaster. Be aware that variations include water-resistant and quick-drying types which will adversely affect drying and paint absorption.

Collage

An assemblage of separate items pasted together to form one artwork.

Copper adhesive tape

Used by stained glass artists for edging cut glass.

Copper paint

A three-part painting process requiring an undercoat, a coat of paint composed of copper paint in suspension, and a verdigris patina to develop oxidation, so changing the colour from copper to blue green.

Corrugated board

Ribbed board usually used for boxes and packaging. Coloured board available for decorative use.

Decoupage

The art of cutting, pasting and varnishing flat images to decorate items.

Embossing

Raised surface design in relief – the opposite of engraving. Embossing adds matter, texture or lines to a surface with adhesive or a tool.

Embossing powder

Resin powders which adhere to wet paint or size and are cured by direct heat, e.g. from a heat gun or element. Once cured they change, melting dull grains to a shiny, raised coating.

Encaustic wax

Compound of beeswax, pigment and dammar resin. Harder finish than beeswax. Can be used for encaustic (wax) painting or as a collage medium, adhesive and/or sealant. Wide range of colours also available.

Fabric paint

Fabric paints, including puff and sun paints, are basically acrylic and available as transparent or opaque colours. Extender or fabric paint base (medium) will render colours more transparent. Can be used on most supports as long as they are sealed correctly. Have a tendency to fade.

Fixative

Spray to seal artwork. Stops media such as charcoal and pastels from smudging.

Flocking

Small fibre particles glued to a surface for colour and textural purposes with a velvet finish.

Foil – usually metallic

Thin, film-backed material, adds sparkle and interest. Comes in a variety of colours and finishes. Applied onto glue or fusible web and then backing peeled away.

Fusible web (hot fuse webbing or appliqué paper)

Comes with or without paper backing. Conventionally used to fuse fabrics together. Webbed form of glue that melts when heated. Can be painted and cut into shapes. Cover with non-stick paper before fusing to the support with a hot iron. May be overlaid with more painted web, lutradur, foils or stitching for detail and definition.

Gel medium

Versatile acrylic medium. Appears white but dries clear. Is intended to mix with acrylic paint to add density. Can also be used to do transfers and as a sealant. If applied thickly, shrinks when dry unless mixed with paint. Very flexible so suitable for any support. Has similar properties to texture paste.

Gesso

A primer consisting of gypsum (Plaster of Paris) and chalk with a binding medium – traditionally rabbit skin granules. Used for priming canvases, paper or coating wooden panels prior to painting. Can be scratched into or added to water-based paint for texture.

Gilding paste

Wax-based metallic paste used to highlight texture. Solvent is turpentine.

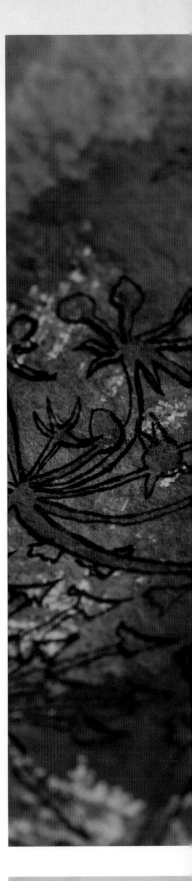

Gilder's milk or size

Various products which adhere metal leaf to a substrate. A simple 'milk' is made by thinning tacky or stencil glue with water to a thin cream – or simply use neat.

Glaze

From the word glass, in painting terminology refers to a transparent medium. Coloured glazes are made by thinning paint with relevant solvents and sometimes, in the case of acrylics, neutral retarder added to delay drying time. Can be applied over previously painted areas to modify colour or texture.

Glitter

Minuscule metal-like flakes that add shimmer and sparkle.

Hake brush

Ultra soft goat-hair brush with long, flat handle. Used for blending and laying in large areas of watery colour or absorbing excess colour. Not to be confused with a varnish brush.

Heat gun

Electric heating tool, similar to a hairdryer, but running at much higher temperatures. Industrial strength used for removing paint, melting plastics and solder; craft version commonly used in stamping for melting embossing powder and shrinking plastics.

Hog-hair brush

Standard grade, economical, natural bristle brush, commonly used for oil or acrylic paint. Available in flat or round form and in a large range of sizes.

Ink-jet printer

Most common type of home printer. Semi-permanent ink. Images not waterproof unless fixed with fixative or clear lacquer.

Interfacing – iron-on

Fusible interfacing accepts most paint types on unglued side. Creates soft effect similar to thin felt. Cut and fuse painted interfacing with an iron to support.

Linseed oil

Pressed from linseeds – the common base for oil paints and scumble glaze. Boiled linseed oil dries faster than raw linseed oil, but yellows with age. Refined artists' variety is clearer and used for making and thinning artists' oil colours.

Lacquer spray

Clear spray varnish. Available in gloss, satin or matt.

Lutradur

A non-woven polyester fibre. Looks like dressmaker's interfacing. Comes in different weights and colours. Can be painted, dyed, printed, stamped, stencilled, printed on with an ink-jet printer and stitched, etc. Reacts to heat, creating distressed effects. The web disintegrates to a fine mesh. Thick paint acts as a resist to heat, burning slowest. Will react differently depending on whether it is coloured before or after distressing, and depending on type of medium applied. If heated when damp the surface will remain flat. Applied to support with fusible web, glue or stitching.

Masonite (hardboard)

Pressed fibre board commonly used for construction. Available in standard thicknesses from 3mm up, smooth on one side and may be pre-coated (white). Rough side has canvas-like pattern imprinted which, when primed, makes cheap substitute for painting canvases. Pegboard is masonite drilled with holes in a grid pattern.

Matt/Matte

Flat, lustreless or dull – non-reflective.

Matt medium

Versatile acrylic medium to make shiny surfaces appear matt. May also be used as an adhesive and as an acrylic retarder.

MDF (medium density fibre board) /Supawood

Manufactured boards from wood fibres, wax and resin bonded at high temperature and pressure. Denser than hardboard or plywood, easy to cut accurately, smooth on both sides. Available in various standard thicknesses.

Metal leaf

Whisper-thin sheets of metallic foil used with a glue binder (gilding milk or size), to add lustrous highlights to any surface. Sold in booklets with tissue interleaving. Range from expensive 9ct gold to Dutch metal, aluminium, copper and variegated colour. Leaf fragments known as skewings. Varnish with shellac or spray lacquer.

Metallic powders

Metal dust particles suspended in or blown onto wet paint or varnish for shiny effects. Range from gold through silver, copper and bronze.

Methylated spirits

Methyl alcohol – a type of denatured alcohol. Solvent for shellac flakes, as well as for some quick-drying, spirit-based paints, e.g. glass paint. Used in solvent release paint techniques.

Mineral turpentine

Also known as white spirits, chemically based on natural turpentine from resin of pine trees. Used for diluting and cleaning oil and enamel paint. Refined artists turpentine used as a medium on its own or with artists' linseed oil for glazing or thinning oil paints. To recycle allow to stand. Sediment settles allowing clean liquid to be poured off and reused. Never throw turpentine down a drain.

Mount board

Thick board used for mounting and framing artwork. May also be used as a support for mixed media. Available in many colours.

Negative stencil

Block-out or mask painted around or over, and when removed reveals a negative or blank shape.

Non-stick sheet

Heatproof silicone pressing sheet for ironing. Does not stick to adhesives. Protects delicate materials from heat.

Oil paint

Traditionally made from seed oils and finely ground pigment. Differ considerably from the house painting enamels in terms of quality and quantity of pigment to binder ratio. Different pigments have different properties: some are more saturated. Graded according to light-fastness and transparency reflected by codes on tubes. Take a long time to dry unless mixed with synthetic mediums. Artists' turpentine and seed oils are used for thinning and making glazes, mineral turpentine solvent for cleaning equipment (will leave paint finish dull if used for thinning).

Oil paint mediums

Resin and synthetic alkyd based, considerably speed up drying time when mixed with oil paint.

Paint stick

Oil paint made from drying oils blended with pigment and moulded into sticks. Self-seal with a skin that must be rubbed off before use.

Palette knife

Usually small, trowel-like knife or spatula for mixing, applying and spreading paint and other textural mediums.

Paste paper

Paper coated with paste made from cooking 1 part flour, 1 part sugar and 2 parts water with addition of a pinch of ground cloves as a pest deterrent. May be coloured with acrylic paints or inks. Used for textural effects.

Patina

Sheen on any surface produced by age and use or chemical activator to produce that effect.

Pearlescent pigment powder

Finely ground mica (shine) and pigment (colour).

Pewter

Soft metal alloy of tin, copper and zinc, among others. Easily malleable, can be cut with scissors and tooled by embossing or engraving. Can be left shiny or darkened with patina and polished for an antique finished.

Photocopy

Duplicate image made on a machine – may be enlarged or reduced. Toner based images suitable for image transfers (solvent is thinners).

Pigment powder

Finely ground oxides or minerals for colouring paint and plaster.

Plaster of Paris

Fine white form of heat-treated gypsum plaster. Sets very quickly; can be used for moulds or thinned for self-levelling plaster. Re-enforced with bandage (or other matrices) for casts. The main ingredient in gesso.

Prime

To give wood a base coat for subsequent coats to bond.

Printing plate

a) Broad term for a surface that carries an image to be printed. Applied directly to support. Image to be printed may be raised, carved or flush with the surface.

b) Non-absorbent surface can be coated with paint or ink from which to take a print.

Puff paint (dimensional or expandable paint)

When heated with a hairdryer, expands or puffs up like popcorn. To create a velvet effect, blot with paper towel, cover with baking paper and iron. Can be worked on with gilding, paint sticks, etc., to enhance texture.

Resists

Broad term for impenetrable barrier inhibiting the flow of paint or other medium onto the working surface.

Retarder or retarder gel (acrylics)

Transparent acrylic base to extend (retard) drying time of acrylic paint. Also known as acrylic extender.

Rollers

Tubular paint applicators (sponge, wool, mohair and synthetic fibres), attached to a handle.

Scrapers

Any flat implement (including credit-type cards, commercial paint scrapers, palette knives, tile glue applicators, plastic knives and hard pieces of card) to apply mediums in thin layers or scrape surfaces.

Shapers

Tools with similar handles to paintbrushes but with rubber or silicone tips in different sizes, shapes and degrees of firmness. Many uses with paint and clay. Particularly used for blending, shaping and fine scraping.

Shellac

Resin varnish, produced from the secretion of the lac insect, sold in flakes or liquid form. Dissolves in denatured alcohol. Quick-drying. Recommended varnish for gilding as it prevents tarnishing. Highly toxic, with a strong odour.

Silk (sun) paint

Water or alcohol based paints and pigment dyes in a brilliant colour range, conventionally used on silk or watercolour paper. Develop intensity when exposed to bright sunlight.

Spray Paint

Solvent based, liquid paints in cans under pressure with nozzles for easy spray application. Commercial spray paint is available in many finishes including enamel, antique, hammered, metallic, webbing and a wide range of colours including neon and fluorescent.

Stencil

Simple shape or window cut out of card, plastic or metal. Single stencil: complete design on one sheet. More complex and multiple stencils have separate windows. Positive stencil: window through which a medium is applied. See negative stencil.

Stencil brush

Brush with round, tightly packed head of bristles, all cut to the same level.

Stencil glue

Similar to contact adhesive, doesn't dry out, remains tacky. Water soluble while wet, requires thinners as solvent when dry. Enables items to be repositioned without permanently bonding them. Creates tacky surfaces, e.g. for stencils, printing tables, photographs and picture framing. Available as spray mount glue in cans.

Texture paste

Also sold as modelling paste, may be applied to any surface for an impasto finish. Available in smooth, textured or fancy finishes. Flexible and strong enough to hold objects impressed into it, may shrink on drying.

Thinners

Solvent and cleaner for lacquer products, extremely strong, rapidly deteriorates many surfaces and fabrics. Removes adhesive residues.

Thumbnails

Small drawings to sketch ideas or low resolution photographic images.

Transfers

Transfer of images from one support to another. Multiple methods.

Tyvek

Looks and feels like thick paper. Not as absorbent. Comes in sheet form in three different weights. Acts primarily like paper so media and techniques used are the same as paper. Distorted by heating with an iron or heat gun (less predictable). Painting, which side it's heated and length of heating will create different effects. Can be used in photocopiers and computer printers that do not use heat.

Varnish

Generic term referring to general sealer. Varnishes range from mineral-spirit based polyurethanes to more popular water-based varieties. Available in clear, tinted, gloss, semi-gloss, satin or matt (suede) finish.

Varnish brush

Flat, broad bristles brush for light wash application.

Wallpaper paste

Granules, needing to be softened in water becoming a non-sticky glue. Suitable for paper work. Slow drying thus facilitating repositioning. Dried paper can be lifted by soaking in water.

Heartful thanks

I may not have gone where I intended to go, but I think I have ended up where I intended to be.

Douglas Adams

Heartful thanks to my dear co-author, Monique, for motivating and managing me in the media mix – this book would not have happened without you! And Angie, for keeping me on my toes!

Mom, I know you would have been proud of this one too. Michael, your practical help (especially with photography) and sensitive support, I couldn't be without. Zera and Joshua – thanks for the inspiration, constructive crits and tea! – Josh, thanks for Control F! Sue, Moira and Shelagh – thanks for listening. Special thanks to all 'my ladies' for being so tolerant. Gail and Maureen, your paintings for backgrounds were most useful. Nondomiso, I am ever grateful for your cleaning skills.

Peter for your love, care and creativity - and my wonderful workshop. Mom, for sponsoring such an inspiring trip to New Zealand. John for the generous loan of the camera. Liz and Gem for organising yourselves and occasional meals. Lindsay and Sarie for support, interest and keeping Carrie happy. Melinda and Martin, all the Louws and Zelda for being friends indeed, Robyn Logan for encouraging my first efforts, Lynn and Malcolm for smoothing my move. Sue, Rod, Clara, Anthony, Liz and all my other friends and family for bearing with me – you know who you are! Special thanks to Christopher for your most constructive help.

Monean Winterbach for all your promotions past and present. Helen Sunde and the Fowls for your kind sponsorship. Val and Andre Roux for mountboards and old journal. Sandy Griffiths for finding the bits and pieces. Yolande and Manfred Kulemann of Art on Main for your enthusiastic support and advice.

As ever, thanks to our Artful team:
Wilsia Metz for your part in our Art
Lindie Metz for producing the goods on time!
Liezl Maree for your patience in packaging our projects to perfection
Ivan Naudé for your ultra smart visual art
And Annlerie van Rooyen for getting our translation down to a fine art.